Reviews

"Whether music is your ___ or avocation, you will enjoy reading *Musical Laughs*. In addition to the woodwind and conductor jokes, I loved the nod to athletes and Major Giggles. Thanks, Pat, for reminding us that laughter is the best medicine."

—**Robert Calonico** *(Clarinet), Director of Bands Emeritus, University of California at Berkeley; Music Director and Conductor of the Golden Gate Park Band, San Francisco, CA and of the Danville Community Band, Danville, CA*

"While playing in a musical organization is a very serious business, musicians have always softened the tension with jokes about themselves, their instruments and especially conductors. Patricia Wheeler has been collecting such jokes for over thirty years, and now has made a large selection available to everyone through her *Musical Laughs*. In addition to the old classics, like "What do you call someone who hangs around with musicians? A drummer" or "Why do clarinetists (also used for violists and saxophonists) put their cases on the dashboards? So they can park in the handicapped zone," there are many interesting musical connections, such as famous people or cities with musical names. And of course, there are the "knock, knock" and the many "student excuses for not practicing" jokes. So, *Brighten Up Your Day* with Wheeler's *Musical Laughs*."

—**Raoul F Camus** *(French Horn), Director Emeritus of the Queens Symphonic Band; Professor Emeritus, The City University of New York, NY*

"This book is the perfect antidote for these difficult days. It is chocked full of everything from one-liners to groaners to jokes we may have heard somewhere along the line during our careers/avocations as musicians. I could identify with the joke about how many flutists it takes to change a lightbulb. This would make a great gift for fellow musician friends."

—**Nan Raphael** *(Piccolo/Flute), Freelancer, Piccolist with the Washington Winds Recording studio band, the International Flute Orchestra, and the Capitol City Symphony; Former Piccoloist with the US Army Field Band, Washington, DC*

"Throughout her lifelong love of music, Pat Wheeler has lived up to her motto, "No Fun without Music, No Music without Fun." To that extent, she has compiled a plethora of musical jokes and anecdotes that will delight, surprise, shock and perhaps even appall her readers—but never bore them! Anyone who understands the humorous side of music making will be entertained for hours."

—*Art Himmelberger (Percussion), Past-President of the Association of Concert Bands; Recipient of Kappa Kappa Psi's Distinguished Service to Music Medal Award; Director of Music, Marist College, Poughkeepsie, NY*

"Pat's compendium is likely the most comprehensive collection of musical jokes, puns, and riddles I have ever seen. This tome will keep you entertained for hours. I highly recommend it."

—*Tony Clements (Tuba), Principal Tubist and soloist, Symphony Silicon Valley, San Jose, CA; Conductor of four instrumental groups at Ohlone College, Fremont, CA; Brass Instructor, Stanford University, Palo Alto, CA*

"The laughs, the wordplays, and the truth in these pages...I chuckle as I think about all the people and the personalities that they represent...I just hope none of them are about me!! I know everyone will smile, enjoy, and even share these jokes!"

—*Adam Frey (Euphonium), International Euphonium Soloist; Associate Professor of Music, University of North Georgia, Dahlonega, GA*

"*Musical Laughs* is a delight! Clever and often side-splittingly funny, this joyful collection took me down memory lane and introduced me to many new humorous musical twists. No one is spared, from contrabassoons to conductors, band directors to Beethoven, the joke is on us all! A great reminder to find the fun, and laugh at ourselves. I really enjoyed it."

—*Lara Webber (Voice), formerly Associate Conductor of the Baltimore (MD) Symphony Orchestra and Charleston (SC) Symphony Orchestra and Music Director of the Charleston Symphony Orchestra Chorus; currently Conductor and Music Director, Livermore-Amador Symphony, Livermore, CA*

"For most of my life, I have had two great passions: music and dad jokes. *Musical Laughs* by Pat Wheeler combines those two loves, and has left me very satisfied. Now I have a new arsenal of humor for my friends and family, thanks to this book. I especially appreciate the lines about quirky guitarists like myself. Music does many things. It can draw out deep feelings, thoughts and memories. It can have enormous depth and meaning. It can make us weep, and yes, it certainly can make us laugh. I am very fortunate to be in a profession that allows me to remind people of the things that make life beautiful, like music and laughter. For anyone looking to spend some time immersed in those two elements, I highly recommend this book. Thank you, Pat Wheeler, for sharing your funny sense of humor with us."

—*Chris Carter (Guitar), Executive Director, Livermore Valley Performing Arts Center, Livermore, CA*

"A book full of wonderful musical quips, jokes and lists for music lovers who love lists. Funny book with tidbits of information and facts to give you a good chuckle."

—*Bryan K. Holbrook (Saxophone), Music Teacher/ Instrumental Music Coordinator, Hayward Unified School District, Hayward, CA*

"This book is going to tickle the fancy of many musicians. The beginning musician will come to know the joy of playing music with other musicians."

—*Madeliene E. Ward (Bassoon), Music Teacher (retired), Grades K-8, Sunol, CA*

"*Musical Laughs* is a delightful collection of musical jokes and riddles for all. I especially liked the woodwind jokes and the Classical Chuckles chapter. This is a fun book about the musical world that will uplift your spirits and brighten your day."

—*Karla Angle (Flute), Elementary School Band and Orchestra Director, Danville and Alamo, CA; Director of the Flute Fest Flute Ensemble, Danville, CA*

"WOW! As a teacher of private music lessons and a band director for nearly a half century, I thought I'd heard and retold 'em all! Patricia's *Musical Laughs* disabused me of that notion! There are many in this book that I have never heard of in all my years in music, but others are very familiar."

—*Mike Brosius (Accordion, Banjo, Ukulele, Cimbasso), formerly Band Director: Grades 5-8 in Tracy and Livermore, CA and Grades 9-12 in Santa Ana, CA and Trinidad, CO; Jazz Band Director at Trinidad State Junior College, Trinidad, CO; currently Teacher of private music lessons and gigs, Silver City, NM*

"Congratulations on creating *Musical Laughs*, the joke book every musician says they will write, but doesn't! Shared and laughed with my family at the silly, fun and often times true jokes and stories found within. We love your book, it's hard to put down. Your *Musical Laughs* certainly 'brightened up our day'!

—*Cindy Browne Rosefield (Upright and Electric Bass), Director of Instrumental Music and Director of the Jazz Ensemble, Las Positas College, Livermore, CA*

"This book covers all kinds of music, including circus music. Some think of circus music as a serious part of the act when we had live bands at the circus. This book shows the humorous side of it too. Keep an eye out for this book and have a fun time reading it."

—*Charlie Bennett (Cornet), Circus Music Historian and Founder of the Windjammers Unlimited, Wichita, KS*

MUSICAL LAUGHS

Other Books by Patricia H. Wheeler, PhD

Successful Tails: The Wonders of Therapy Dogs

Therapy Dogs in Action: Their Stories of Service and Love

Amazon, The Golden Eagle: Her Story of Overcoming a Tough Start

Musical
LAUGHS

Notes to Brighten Up Your Day

PATRICIA H. WHEELER, PhD

Illustrated by Rebecca P. Wheeler

LUMINARE PRESS

WWW.LUMINAREPRESS.COM

Illustrations by Rebecca P. Wheeler

Categories for searches—1. Humor—Music, 2. Jokes—Music, 3. Music—Jokes

Printed in the United States of America

Luminare Press
442 Charnelton St.
Eugene, OR 97401
www.luminarepress.com

LCCN: 2021904932
ISBN: 978-1-64388-577-3

Dedication

*To my patient and tolerant music teachers and conductors—
among them, Evan Bollinger, John Thomas, John Kinyon,
Ward Woodbury, Guido Fazio, Jay Roberts, Bob Williams,
Chuck Taber, David Turner, Leland Lillehaug, Col. John
R. Bourgeois, Bernie Berke, Cindy Browne Rosefield, Cheryl
Woldseth, Norman Dea, Scott Lycan, Larry Colon, Bryan
Holbrook, Lawrence Anderson, Bob Calonico, Karla Angle,
Tony Clements, Dan Smith—and all my fellow band members
from junior high school on to today's community bands.*

*Also, to the residents and business people of Talent, Oregon,
who lost so much in the September 2020 wildfires and the
firefighters who tried so hard to save their town.*

Contents

Preface

Two requirements for learning to play a musical instrument well or to be a serious singer are (1) practicing and (2) a sense of humor. Listen to yourself! Others have to listen to you unless you are in solitary confinement. And pity your poor teachers. I have such admiration for music teachers. Without their patience and perseverance, none of us would be where we are today, even if all we do now is listen to others perform and appreciate music.

For over 30 years, I have been writing and collecting music jokes. It started so I could use them as fillers in the newsletters that I did for the Pleasanton Community Concert Band and other groups. Then many members of that band and other music groups started sending me jokes. At several rehearsals, things happened that gave me more ideas for jokes. Suddenly I had many scores of them. With all my other activities, all I could do was put them in a folder on my computer. What to do with all of them?

In the spring of 1997, I went with the Community Band at Sea trip in the Caribbean on the SS Norway. I shared many of the jokes I had collected with people in that group. They enjoyed them and told me more jokes. But the decision to revise what I had collected, write many more, and publish a book in the future came on the flight from Miami to Dallas on my way home to California from that cruise. I was chatting with the woman sitting next to me. After telling her about our band cruise, she mentioned that she had played clarinet in high school, but never kept it up. I told her a couple clarinet jokes. She chuckled and seemed to enjoy them. When she asked if I had more jokes, I went into the depths of the overhead rack and pulled out several pages worth. She stuffed her airline magazine back into the seat pocket and started reading the jokes. She laughed and laughed. Her laughing was getting louder and louder. Her daughter, who was sitting behind her, asked, "Mom, are you okay?" She replied, "Just great!" After about ten pages, she exclaimed, "You need to publish a book of musician jokes. These are great! All you need is an illustrator." She had mentioned earlier that she taught art for a while, so I invited her to be the illustrator. She said, "Oh, I only do oils and portraits. They just wouldn't fit in a joke book."

While working on a project in Newark, New Jersey, I met a high school administrator who had been a coach. I told him about the book. He said, "You need a section in there about musical athletes because that will attract a whole new audience." Soon after that he sent me a two-page list of musical athletes, starting with Doug Flutie and Brian Piccolo since he knew I played those two instruments.

Musical last names caught my eye when reading newspaper articles and obituaries. I collected about 100 of them and shared them with a friend of mine who was not a musician, but a music lover who regularly attended both the San Francisco Symphony and the San Francisco Opera. She laughed the entire time going down the list and added more. I expanded that by looking in telephone books (the printed versions we used to have), alumni directories, and more newspapers.

While driving home from my younger son's home in Eugene, Oregon, I went through Talent, Oregon. I thought that would be a great place for musicians to live. Soon I came to Hornbrook, California. The list of such places was underway. Before I knew it, I had hundreds of them. Many starting with Bell...and Rock.... But I cut the list way down so it wouldn't take up too much space in the book. And that was true of the other lists in this book.

I have many lists in my life, the "Chopin" list, which gets much shorter each time I go to the store and then it starts growing again. Then there is the "Toodle" list, which rarely has things crossed off, but grows on a regular basis.

All these jokes sat in folders on my computer for years, with my occasionally adding more and starting twice to assemble them into a book. But I never seemed to have time to finish a book with all the other things in my life. Then came the shelter-at-home order on March 17, 2020, with the coronavirus. I had plenty to do at home, with piles of papers and music to go through that I had accumulated over the years, as well as lots of photos and emails. And much more on my "Toodle" list.

I needed some humor in my life at this time. I got lots of comforting and loving from my dogs, and enjoyed nature programs on TV and listening to quiet music in the background. I needed to laugh though. That need lead me back to the folders filled with music jokes. I started editing them and sorting them to compile a joke book. This resulted in my preparing a draft of *Musical Laughs*. Now I can share them with you. I hope you find it beneficial whenever you need a laugh. Laughs are good medicine, as we know. Read a few each day. Enjoy them. And don't forget to take deep breaths from the diaphragm.

PATRICIA H. WHEELER, PHD

Acknowledgements

I appreciate so much the assistance provided by the following people in my being able to finish this book and reaching my goal of completing it for decades—

Mike Brosius who supported my work on the earlier drafts of the book (1997 and 2013) as well as this version

Joelyn Rose and Madeliene Ward who worked with me extensively on the first draft of this version

Tony Altwies, Jomi Coffield, Jim Otto, Sandy Shepard, Dan Smith, Yong Suh, and Craig Wilson who answered cover design and content-related questions for me

Rebecca P. Wheeler for doing the illustrations for the book

The people who provided review statements for this book, several of whom pointed out needed corrections and sent me additional jokes

And especially the people at Luminare Press: Patricia Marshall, Owner, whose enthusiasm for this book spurred me on; Kim Harper-Kennedy, Project and Operations Manager, who kept things moving along; and Kristen Brack, Graphic Designer, who took my rough drafts and turned them into this book while putting up with all my requests for changes and additions.

This book would never have been completed without the support of all these people.

1

Take Note

How many musician jokes are there?

Just one. All the rest are true. See if you can find that one joke!

———

These jokes are so bad, you may not be able to Handel them. You may Wonder Ver-di came from. You may feel some are too Franck, or that they are for the Byrds. Others are a lot of Bull. They may make you Liszt-less. They can become too Mendelssohn. If you can't get through them, you had better go Haydn out Bach before you un-Ravel. But if you get through them, you'll be in a state of Bliss.

———

Joan: Why would a violinist play *A Minor Concerto for Violin* when she could play *A Major Concerto for Violin*?

Josh: She doesn't want to become famous too quickly.

———

What do a piano and a school custodian have in common?
They both have hammers and 88 keys.

I asked for a piano player, not a player piano.

Student: Why are brass players so confused when they switch instruments?

Professor Julliardo: When they play trumpet, they use three fingers; for euphonium they use four fingers; and for tuba as many as five fingers; but if they pick up the trombone, they have seven positions to play.

Why do clarinetists put their cases on the dashboards?

So they can park in the handicapped zone and get to rehearsal on time.

Patricia H. Wheeler

What do a trombonist and a Roto-Rooter person have in common?

> They both know how to use a snake to clean out smelly pipes.

How does Professor Julliardo decide who will be the principal oboist?

> He sends all the oboists in for hearing tests and picks the one that is most auditorily-challenged.

What do bassoonists and jailers have in common?

> They both look after crooks.

Why are cornet players so good at bridge?

> Because they know how to trump-it.

What was the favorite song of Oedipus Rex?

> "I Want a Girl Just Like the Girl Who Married Dear Old Dad."

What do a flügelhorn player and an auto mechanic have in common?

> They both have to deal with sticky valves.

Why didn't the musician want to handle the sheet music?

> He was afraid he would get a staph infection.

How can you get rid of an old tenor sax?

> Leave it in a McDonald's parking lot.

What did the flutist play to the pet store owner?

> "How Much Is That Doggie in the Window?"

If you are driving on a narrow, dark country road late at night and see a saxophone player and a conductor in the road ahead and cannot avoid hitting both of them, which one do you hit first?

> The conductor, business before pleasure.

What starts when you decide to become a serious clarinet player?

> The nightmare of the reeds.

How many bassoonists does it take to tile a kitchen floor?

> Depends on how tall they are and how thin you slice them, but be forewarned that the health and police departments might not like it.

Musical Chairs

Sometimes it is hard to get everything together for our performance, especially when we undertake an opera. We were performing Richard Wagner's opera *Siegfried*, which calls for a horn solo played off stage so as to sound as if it were coming from some distance away. Since the hornist couldn't see the conductor, he instructed her to count the measures carefully in order to come in at the precise time. On the performance night, when the time came for the horn solo, the hornist began exactly at the right time. All of us could hear the sounds of a distant horn. Then, suddenly there was a sour sound, a loud crash, a thud, and then…silence. The conductor was outraged and, at the end of the act, rushed off stage to find the hornist. "Maestro," she said. "Before you say anything, you're not going to believe what happened. You know I came in at the right time, and everything was going so well, when, suddenly, this enormous stagehand ran up, grabbed my horn, threw it to the side, and pushed me down, saying, 'Stop that, you dummy! Don't you know there's a performance going on out there and people are trying to sing?'"

Why did Bill Clinton learn to play tenor sax?

> So he would be real smooth, could improvise on the spot, and would be seen as a man of culture.

What is the difference between a jazz saxophonist and an AK-47?

> The AK-47 only repeats 600 times a minute.

Did you hear about the guitarists who collaborated on a book of chords?

> Each contributed only one.

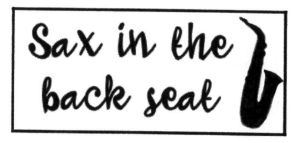

What do a horn player and a stunt pilot have in common?

> They love twists and turns.

What do young rock and roll drummers do?

> Flail and wail.

Patricia H. Wheeler

What did the student who wanted to learn to march do when he was told he couldn't be in Professor Julliardo's marching band?

He joined the Army.

Which instrument made the beep-beep sound toward the end of the third piece on the band's program?

The trumpet player's pager.

What kind of music critic would you prefer for your band's concert?

(a) One who bases her article on what pieces the publicity says you will be playing.

(b) One who bases her article on how your band played at its second rehearsal.

(c) One who bases her review on what the conductor says after the concert.

(d) One who bases it on what she overhears the audience members who leave early say on their way out.

(e) One who bases her review on what she thinks you should have played at the concert.

(f) One who doesn't come to your concert, but writes a review anyway.

Hope you have a more objective critic than these.

If you were lost in the woods and came across three people, which one would you trust for directions:—the one who says he's an in-tune tenor sax player, the one who admits to being an out-of-tune tenor sax player, or the one who claims to be Santa Claus?

The out-of-tune tenor sax player. The other two have been hallucinating.

Some Vehicles for Musicians

Auburn Speedster

Buick Encore

Chevy Traverse

Chrysler Custom Imperial Airflow

Fiat 130 Opera

Gig Boat

Isotta Fraschini 8A/Bass

Mitsubishi Galant

Dodge Pickup

Patricia H. Wheeler

What do both percussionists and carpenters use?

Wood blocks.

What does your band have if it has a very large horn section?

A lot of bulls.

Who is the nerd in the orchestra?

The member who owns his own contrabassoon.

Why did Strauss entitle his comic opera, *Die Fledermaus*?

Because it's about a flying rodent that takes the air out of blimps.

Why is it illegal to play bassoons on the beach?

Because if it's foggy, all the boats will crash.

What do musicians like to do in the summer?

(a) Listen to ukulele bands and lei around.

(b) Practice day and night at music camp.

(c) Play volleyball with The Beach Boys.

(d) March in all the summer parades.

All of the above, unless they are the really stuffy types.

Top ten reasons for bringing a kazoo to work:

(10) Your boss won't let you practice your trombone at work.

(9) Your band director said to always be ready to perform.

(8) It's like a zoo at work.

(7) You can leave meaningful messages on other people's answering machines.

(6) You don't have to listen to the office gossip.

(5) You have an excuse for not answering the phone.

(4) You won't get invited to meetings.

(3) It beats elevator music.

(2) You can carry a tune to accompany your boss' snoring.

(1) It can double as a coffee stirrer.

What can you find in the pasture and in the percussionist's kit?
Cow bells.

Why do they put the orchestra in the pit? Are they that bad?
They play okay, but they're really ugly looking and need to be out of view of the audience.

Some Places for Musicians to Live

Alto, New Mexico

Bell City, Missouri

Bighorn, Montana

Brasstown, North Carolina

Coolville, Ohio

Gig Harbor, Washington

Horn Lake, Mississippi

Little Rock, South Carolina

Pickstown, South Dakota

Reading, Massachusetts

Reeds, Missouri

Rock Tavern, New York

Saxton River, Vermont

Stringtown, Oklahoma

What did the tuba player do when he locked his keys in the car?

Climbed out the window.

Which instrument likes to be _____?

(1) Squeezed	(a) Snare drum
(2) Hugged	(b) Bagpipe
(3) Shaken	(c) Harp
(4) Picked on	(d) Tambourine
(5) Hit on the head	(e) Euphonium
(6) Hit by each other	(f) Chimes
(7) Cuddled in your armpit	(g) Sousaphone
(8) Hammered	(h) Crash cymbals
(9) Plucked	(i) Marching tuba
(10) Brushed	(j) Accordion
(11) Resting on your shoulder	(k) Banjo
(12) Wrapped around your body	(l) Timpani

Answers: 1-j, 2-e, 3-d, 4-k, 5-l, 6-h, 7-b, 8-f, 9-c, 10-a, 11-i, 12-g

My parents told me that, while I am stuck at home for on-line schooling, I should learn to play music on the keyboard, so I found some links to music on my computer.

If there is a string bass player and a cellist both lying in the road ahead, which one should you avoid hitting?

It's hard to avoid the cellist because he is so spread out.

What do pipe smokers do when they quit smoking?

Take up oboe or English horn so they can still fidget with things.

What is a tuba for?

A kind of lumber used for framing houses.

How do you get hold of a baritone player?

You-phone-'em.

If you drop a conductor and a watermelon off a tall building at the same time, which will hit the ground first?

Who cares? They're both so seedy.

What do you call a large kazoo?

A wazoo.

2

Symphonic Jocks

Conductors

Bill Belichick (Football) for the Bell Choir
Scotty Bowman (Hockey) for the Symphony and the Band
Pete Carroll (Football) for the Chorus
Matt Harping (Basketball) for the Harp Ensemble

Symphony Sections

Strings

Alex Bowman (Auto Racing)
Brandon Bass (Basketball)
Bruce Bowen (Basketball)
Cedric Bowers (Baseball)
Derrick Turnbow (Baseball)
Dwayne Bowe (Football)
Frank Viola (Baseball)

Justin Bowers (Hockey)
Kevin Bass (Football)
Korey Stringer (Football)
Lou Stringer (Baseball)
Matt Bowman (Baseball)
Nanci Bowen (Golf)
NaVorro Bowman (Football)
Pedro Viola (Baseball)
Rick Bowness (Hockey)
Russell Bowie (Hockey)
Scott Bower (Soccer)
Scotty Bowman (Hockey)
Travis Bowyer (Baseball)
Zack Bowman (Football)

Woodwinds

Addison Reed (Baseball)
Al Woods (Football)
Andre Reed (Football)
Brian Piccolo (Football)
Chastity Reed (Basketball)
Chris Woods (Soccer)
D'Andre Reed (Football)
Doug Flutie (Football)
Ed Reed (Football)
Jake Reed (Football)
James Reed (Football)
Jeff Reed (Football)
Jeremy Reed (Baseball)
Jerome Woods (Football)
Jim Reed (Auto Racing)

Woodwinds (continued)

Kendrell Reed (Football)
Kerry Wood (Baseball)
Le Var Woods (Football)
Manny Trillo (Baseball)
Patrick Reed (Golf)
Rashaun Woods (Football)
Reed Johnson (Baseball)
Rick Reed (Baseball)
Shirley Englehorn (Golf)
Tiger Woods (Golf)
Willis Reed (Basketball)

Brass

Bob Horner (Baseball)
Brad Cornett (Baseball)
Chris Horn (Football)
George Bone (Baseball)
Jeff Hornacek (Basketball)
Jeff Mutis (Baseball)
Jeremy Horne (Football)
Joel Horner (Baseball)
Keith Van Horne (Basketball)
Kelsey Bone (Basketball)
Lindsey Horan (Soccer)
Mark Bellhorn (Baseball)
Mistie Bass (Basketball)
Patric Hornqvist (Hockey)
Paul Hornung (Football)
Red Horner (Hockey)

Rick Mahorn (Basketball)
Ricky Bones (Baseball)
Roger Hornsby (Baseball)
Sam Horn (Baseball)
Sam Hornish (Auto Racing)

Percussion

Boomer Esiason (Football)
C.J. Beathard (Football)
Cameron Triangle (Golf)
Clay Timpner (Baseball)
Crash Davis (Baseball)
Damian Rolls (Baseball)
Desmond Beatty (Baseball)
Drummond Brown (Baseball)
Jannon Roland (Basketball)
Jerry Mallett (Baseball)
Jim Ringo (Football)
Keith Drumright (Baseball)
Lake Speed (Auto Racing)
Ryan Snare (Baseball)
Tim Drummond (Baseball)
Wil Trapp (Soccer)

Bands

Bill Pickett (Rodeo Riding)
Carl Pickens (Football)
Cody Pickett (Football)
Cool Papa Bell (Baseball)
Dave Ragone (Football)
Johnny Rocker (Baseball)
Matt Pickens (Soccer)
Pat Rapp (Baseball)
Quentin Jammer (Football)
Radek Bonk (Hockey)
Ron Mix (Football)
Ryan A. Bonk (Golf)
Ryan Pickett (Football)
Steve Sax (Baseball)
Wayne "Tree" Rollins (Basketball)

Chorus

Ahman Carroll (Football)
Brian Carroll (Soccer)
Clay Carroll (Baseball)
DeMarre Carroll (Basketball)
Nick Folk (Football)

Patricia H. Wheeler

Nolan Carroll (Football)
Otis Birdsong (Basketball)
Ryan Vogelsong (Baseball)
Sang Lan (Gymnastics)
Spencer Paysinger (Football)
Vijay Singh (Golf)
Tyler Bass (Football)
Wayne Presley (Hockey)

Bell Choir

Bert Bell (Football)
Bill Ring (Football)
Bobby Bell (Football)
Brad Ring (Soccer)
Byron Bell (Football)
Charlie Bell (Basketball)
Cody Bellinger (Baseball)
Cool Papa Bell (Baseball)
Dave Bing (Basketball)
David Bell (Baseball)
Doug La Belle II (Golf)
Jacob Bell (Football)
Jason Bell (Football)
Jay Bell (Baseball)
Joe Altobelli (Baseball)
Joique Bell (Football)
Kendrell Bell (Football)
Kenisho Bell (Basketball)
Le'Veon Bell (Football)
Mark Bell (Hockey)
Mike Bell (Wrestling)

Bell Choir (continued)

Peggy Kirk Bell (Golf)
Raja Bell (Basketball)
T.J. Bell (Auto Racing)
Tatum Bell (Football)
Walt Bellamy (Basketball)
Yeremiah Bell (Football)

Harp Ensemble

Alan Harper (Football)
Alvin Harper (Football)
Bryce Harper (Baseball)
Chandler Harper (Golf)
Derek Harper (Basketball)
Harry Harper (Baseball)
Laura Harper (Basketball)
Nick Harper (Football)
Roman Harper (Football)
Ron Harper (Basketball)
Ryne Harper (Baseball)
Travis Harper (Baseball)

Notes in Tune

Alena Sharp (Golf)
Bill Sharp (Baseball)
Blas Minor (Baseball)
Brian Keyster (Baseball)
Brady Keyes (Football)
Bud Sharp (Baseball)

Patricia H. Wheeler

Claude Minor (Football)
Damon Minor (Baseball)
Dan Hinote (Hockey)
Darren Sharper (Football)
Dick Van Note (Football)
Dwight Scales (Football)
Frank Gracesqui (Baseball)
Jack Flater (Baseball)
Jamie Sharper (Football)
Jimmy Key (Baseball)
Joe Grace (Baseball)
Johnny Majors (Football)
Josh Sharpless (Baseball)
K. B. Sharp (Basketball)
Keyvius Sampson (Baseball)
Leroy Keyes (Football)
Louis Lipps (Football)
Mark Grace (Baseball)
Mike Minor (Baseball)
Patrick Sharp (Hockey)
Rollie Fingers (Baseball)
Ryan Minor (Baseball)
Scott Sharpe (Auto Racing)
Shannon Sharpe (Football)
Sterling Sharpe (Football)
Walter Sharpe (Basketball)

Musical Laughs   21

Dynamic Jocks

Adam Graves (Hockey)
Bryan Bellows (Hockey)
Chet Forte (Basketball)
Matt Forte (Football)
Willie Blair (Baseball)

With the Beat

Brandon Rush (Basketball)
Calvin Pace (Football)
Dit Clapper (Hockey)
Glendon Rusch (Baseball)
Joey Goodspeed (Football)
Kirk Triplet (Golf)
Larry Tripplett (Football)
T.J. Rushing (Football)

Others

Al Toon (Football)
Bart Starr (Football)
Ben Sheets (Baseball))
Bryan Pittman (Football)
David Starr (Auto Racing)
Eric Show (Baseball)
Gary Player (Golf)
Mia Hamm (Soccer)
Rajon Rondo (Basketball)
Reggie Tongue (Football)
Scott Player (Football)
Scotty Pippen (Basketball)

Race Horses for the Parade

Arts and Letters
Belmar
Bluegrass Cat
Concert Tour
Count Fleet
Counterpoint
Dark Star
Day Star
Friar Rock
Keyed Entry
Mad Play
One Count
Real Quiet
Saxon
Stage Door Johnny

How are Symphonic Jocks paid?

By the score.

What teams do musical athletes join?

Charlotte Hornets (Men's Basketball)

Cleveland Rockers (Women's Basketball)

Colorado Rockies (Baseball)

Dallas Stars (Hockey)

Dayton Triangles (Football)

Hartford Dark Blues (Baseball)

Indiana Pacers (Men's Basketball)

Miami Fusion (Soccer)

Rock Island Independents (Football)

St. Louis Blues (Hockey)

San Antonio Stars (Women's Basketball)

Toronto Rock (Lacrosse)

Utah Jazz (Men's Basketball)

Utah Starzz (Women's Basketball)

What do musicians like and baseball pitchers don't like?

Hits.

What do hockey players and drummers have in common?

They both play with sticks.

What do a conductor and a relay racer have in common?

They both have to pass the baton when their turn is up.

What do the horses and drummers in the marching band parade have in common?

> Both need to be harnessed and both mess up our environment.

What do organists and race car drivers have in common?

> Pedal power.

What does the batter use when he can't find his bat?

> His child's clarinet.

What musical instruments do boxers use for their moves?

> A trombone for a fast punch, a tuba for a low blow, a bass drum for a big slam, and a cymbal for a crash.

What do both baseball players and trombonists use?

> Slides.

How can the school band support the track and field team?

It can loan the team equipment—a bassoon for the javelin throw, a cymbal for the discus toss, a hanging tubular bells set for the pole vault, bass drum stands for the hurdle races, a baritone for the hammer throw, and a piccolo for the baton to be handed off to the next runner in a relay race.

What do a flutist and a baseball player have in common?

If they're ready for action and swing too quickly, they can knock out someone's front teeth.

What do you get when you cross a music critic and a bowling ball?

A bowling ball that wouldn't know a good performance if it heard one and a music critic with holes in his head.

What do music groups, baseball batters, and poker players all aim for?

Grand slams.

Why did the oboist join the baseball team?

To learn what a good pitch is.

What is in the repertoire of musical jock groups?

Belle of the Ball	Leroy Anderson, lyrics by Waylon Jennings
Brian's Song	Music by Michael Legrand
Centerfield	John Fogerty
Cheap Seats	Alabama
Going Home	Antonin Dvořák
Joe DiMaggio Done it Again	Woody Guthrie
Michael Row His Boat Ashore	An African-American spiritual
Rodeo	Aaron Copland
Sacrificial Dance from The Rite of Spring	Igor Stravinsky
Surfs Up!	Mychael Danna
Take Me Out to the Ball Game	Albert Von Tilzer
The Ballad of Ichiro Suzuki	Ben Gibbard
The Four Seasons (baseball, football, basketball, hockey)	Antonio Vivaldi
The Greatest	Kenny Rogers
Up, Up and Away	Jimmy Webb
When the Saints Go Marching In	A traditional song
Willie, Mickey and the Duke	Terry Cashman
Yankee Doodle	The Old Guard Fife and Drum Corps
YMCA	Victor Willis

3

Classical Chuckles

Professor Julliardo: Why do you always rush?

Student: To get to the end of the piece first, so I can be first in the class and get an A!

What did the harmonica player get on his music aptitude test?
Drool.

Why did they bury the conductor 20 feet below ground?
Because, deep down, he was a nice guy.

How do you get a gleam in the eyes of an English horn player?
Shine a flashlight in her ear.

Patricia H. Wheeler

Why did the bagpiper frighten the little girl?

> He looked like someone fighting with an octopus, and losing.

Why did Richard Rodgers and Robert Russell Bennett compose *Victory at Sea*?

> (a) To celebrate a successful Coast Guard rescue operation.
>
> (b) To celebrate getting a job with a cruise ship's band.
>
> (c) To honor Charlie, the Tuna, for escaping the fisherman's net.
>
> (d) To celebrate the hurricane changing directions and avoiding their ship.
>
> (e) To honor their friend for catching a great white shark.
>
> (f) To see if they could finish a job together.

Not sure why, but it's wonderful music to listen to and play.

Why do you have to be careful following a musician's pickup truck at night?

Your headlights might reflect off the sousaphone.

What is the problem with people who belong to the handbell choir?

They're all so dingy.

Patient: Will I be able to read music when I get my bifocals?

Optometrist: Sure, why do you ask?

Patient: Because I never could read music before.

What do independent music teachers need?

Appointment secretaries.

How do sax players and guitar players communicate with drummers?

Sax players use notes, whereas guitar players send texts.

Top ten excuses for students not bringing their instrument to rehearsal:

(10) The handle fell off my case.

(9) The instrument wouldn't fit back in the case after I practiced.

(8) I didn't know we were going to play our instruments at rehearsal today.

(7) There wasn't room for both my instrument and my lunch in my case.

(6) I put my instrument in my locker and can't remember the combination.

(5) I put my instrument in my friend's locker and don't know the combination.

(4) My instrument got sick, so I left it in the nurse's office.

(3) My instrument was in the trunk of the car, but when we changed the flat tire on the way to school, I left my instrument by the road.

(2) David Letterman's mom borrowed my instrument for his band.

(1) Bill Clinton borrowed my instrument for his press conference tomorrow so he can toot at the reporters.

How do you know when you are driving past a pawn shop?

By the number of musicians in line at the door.

What do xylophone players and croquet players have in common?

They hit things with hard mallets.

How can you get two piccolo players to play in tune together?

Switch one of them to flute before anyone else notices.

Why is it hard to get good MRIs for drummers?

Because they keep moving their arms and tapping their feet to the beat.

How can you get two piccolo players to play in tune together?

Switch one of them to flute before anyone else notices.

Conductor: Back to bar one.

Tuba player: But my part isn't numbered.

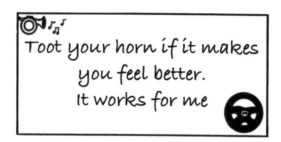

Professor Julliardo: What did you think of the execution of *Madame Butterfly*?

Student: Oh, I didn't realize that she had been killed.

After the concert, the bassoonist was told to pick up his instrument, so he took it out for dinner and a movie.

What do you call a contrabass clarinetist with an IQ above room temperature?

Gifted.

What can violists do, but cellists can't?

Keep their bow end up.

Two men were at a bar. One said, "Hey, I had my IQ checked and it was 175." The other responded, "That's a coincidence; so is mine. What do you do for a living?" "I'm a physicist," was the reply. Again came, "That's a coincidence; so am I." This was overheard at a nearby table and those two compared IQ's at 160 and discovered that both were engineers. At another nearby table, one man despondently said to the other, "Did you heard that? I had my IQ checked and it was 52." The other said, rather enthusiastically, "That's a coincidence; so is mine. What instrument do you play?"

If a flutist and an oboist fall off a tall building at the same time, who will hit the ground first?

> The flutist. The oboist stops part way down to ask for directions.

What do a bad airplane mechanic and a fiddler have in common?

> Both screw up Boeings.

Why does the harpist keep cutting her finger?

> Her "G" string is too sharp.

Why are concert intermissions only 15 minutes long?

> So the clarinetists remember where they were sitting and the drummers don't have to be re-trained.

How can you tell if a guitar player is actually dead?

> Hold out a fifty-dollar bill, but be aware that slight, residual spasmodic plucking actions might occur, even hours after death.

Bruce: Why do you have a cover on the bell of your sousaphone? So people won't hear you?

Mark: No, they can still hear me. But it keeps birds from flying into the bell to look for a good nesting site and also people along the parade route from throwing trash into my horn.

Some Vehicles for Musicians

Alto Teardrop Trailer

Chevy Malibu Classic

Chrysler Airstream

Dodge Ram Big Horn

Ford Freestar

Honda Prelude

Hyundai Sonata

Kia Forte Koup

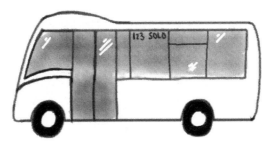

Optare Solo Bus

Why are harpists the highest paid musicians in the orchestra?

Because they know how to pull strings.

Mary: Did you hear about the string bass player who was so bad that even the percussion section noticed?

Sally: Yes. He's playing drums now.

How do you shut up a flutist?

> Shove a pad saver into the flute.

What did the guitar player do when he robbed a music store?

> He ran off with the lute.

What are the major levels of practice?

> Tri-daily, try daily, tri-weekly, try weekly, try weakly, try.

What are the stages in the life of an R&R musician?

> Rattles and resting.
>
> Reading and 'riting.
>
> Rocking and rolling.
>
> Rushing and recuperating.
>
> Reclining and relaxing.

What is another name for *Storm King*?

> El Niño March.

How do you quiet down an electric bass player?

> Put sheet music in front of him.

Patricia H. Wheeler

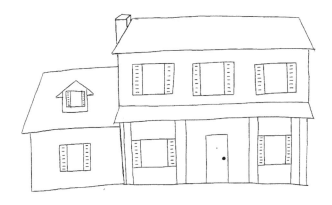

Some Places for Musicians to Live

Bangor, Maine

Bellaire, Minnesota

Brightstar, Arkansas

Crook, Colorado

Dry Run, Ohio

Goosehorn, Tennessee

Hornbrook, California

Lowman, Idaho

Piper, Iowa

Reedsville, Pennsylvania

Rock Valley, Massachusetts

Rush, New York

Sharps, Virginia

Strum, Wisconsin

One of the members of the band called the office asking for the conductor. The secretary informed him that the conductor was dead. The next day, he called again, asking for the conductor. The secretary replied, "I told you yesterday that the conductor is dead." The musician called the next day, again asking for the conductor. The secretary said, "Why do you keep calling here? I already told you the conductor is DEAD!" The band member replied, "I just really enjoy hearing you say that."

How do you keep a harmonica player from starting to play?

Put duct tape over his mouth.

And how do you stop a harmonica player who is already playing?

Hold an aromatic pizza under his nose.

What did the guitar player do when he was told to turn on his amp?

He stroked it gently and sung a love song to it.

Viola player: Did you hear my last performance?

Friend: I hope so!

What is "Stardust"?

The cremated remains of a famous guitarist.

Why did Alex Oppornockity play a whole concert with a flat "B" string on his guitar?

Oppornockity only tunes once.

What did the percussionist do during the music store robbery?

He took a drum and beat it.

What do you call 35 banjo players on a space ship?

A platoon for starting Space War I.

What is the definition of a gentleman?

Someone who knows how to play bagpipes, but keeps them in the closet.

The doctor told the 87-year-old man that if he could get some new organs, he would feel so much better and younger. So, the man rented a larger apartment and bought four organs. But, despite following the doctor's orders, he felt worse. Now he had a $40,000 debt to the music store and $250 more each month for rent payments.

How can you pick out an accordion player at a dinner party?

He is the one with no sense of taste.

What is the difference between rock musicians and government bonds?

Bonds mature.

How are pianists' fingers similar to lightning?

Both rarely strike the same spot twice.

How do you learn to play an electronic keyboard?

Hunt and peck.

Where did the minister send misbehaving choir members?

Sing Sing Prison.

How come Merle Evans could make so much noise on a small cornet?

He had a powerful windpipe.

Professor Julliardo: What happened to *Harold of Italy*?

Student: They cremated him so he would fit into a viola case.

Professor Julliardo was standing on an aluminum ladder waving a metal baton in the middle of the field during a lightning storm, but he wasn't struck by lightning. Why not?

Because he wasn't a good conductor.

4

On A Lighter Note

Name three ways you can use flutes in your yard.

As stakes to hold up plants, as fence posts, or as part of the drip line for your sprinkler system.

We know a student who was so dumb that his music teacher gave him two sticks and made him a drummer, but then he lost one of the sticks and so he became the drum major for the marching band.

What's the difference between a stuck-up euphonium player and a stuck-up piccolo trumpet player?

Two octaves.

How are a woman in labor and an English horn player similar?

They both strain to get something out.

Patricia H. Wheeler

Son: Dad, who is your favorite rock musician?

Dad: Rachmaninoff.

My teacher told me to practice playing chop sticks on the piano.

Why aren't tuba players allowed to marry soprano sax players?
    Their offspring would always play out of tune.

How do you make a clarinet sound like an oboe?
    Sit in front and squawk.

And how do you make an oboe sound like a clarinet?
    Sit in back and squeak.

What has 32 boots and an average IQ of 83?
    A flag corps.

The best version of Haydn's *Trumpet Concerto in E Flat* is "Music Minus One."

What do you call ten conductors at the bottom of the lake?

A good start.

Parent: How can we help send the school's band to Disneyland?

Music Teacher: Get your car washed ten times this weekend.

Who are the intellectuals in our audience?

The ones who are not thinking of the Lone Ranger when the orchestra plays the *William Tell Overture*.

How are a ballistic missile and a disc jockey alike?

Both are easy to fire and you don't know or care where they will land.

What do you call someone who hangs around with musicians?

A drummer-wanna-be.

What is the responsibility of the band's librarian?

Dylan out the music.

What is the difference between an alto clarinetist and a dressmaker?

The dressmaker tucks up the frills.

A man was visiting a cemetery in Europe, when he came across Beethoven's grave. He stopped, and heard *The Ninth Symphony*. Puzzled, he left, but he came back the next day and visited the grave. This time, he heard *The Eighth Symphony*. Again puzzled, he left. On the third day, he returned and heard *The Seventh Symphony*. This time, it intrigued him so much he talked to some people and they decided to have an exhumation. The grave was dug up and when the coffin was opened, there was Beethoven—de-composing!

Two students were asked to play a duet together in a Zoom session. But the sound wasn't synchronized. The teacher had a metronome counting the beats for them, and that made it worse as the students heard the metronome clicks at different times. The only solution seemed to be to have one start a second before the other. But that didn't work either. Zoom classes seem to only be made for playing solos.

Some Places for Musicians to Live

Bass, Alabama

Blue Bell, Pennsylvania

Cross Keys, South Carolina

Drumright, Oklahoma

Fiddletown, California

Grace, Idaho

Horns, Georgia

Melody Hill, Indiana

Pipers Gap, Virginia

Reedy, West Virginia

Rockhouse, Kentucky

Rush City, Minnesota

Sharpsville, Indiana

Tuba City, Arizona

Patricia H. Wheeler

Why did Bach have 20 kids?

> Some say it is because he had no stops on his organ, but the real reason is he wanted to have a full score.

How are a bassoon and an oboe alike?

> Both are ill-winds that no one can blow well.

When does an English horn become a French horn?

> When you pass the halfway point in the Chunnel.

How many clarinets does it take to cover a roof?

> Depends on the size of the roof, but keep in mind that clarinets are apt to leak.

What is the difference between how keyboarders and drummers install their car radios?

> Keyboarders stop the car first.

What does the band manager do if she has a bari sax part to be covered, but no bari sax players?

> Transfers the extra contralto clarinet players to the bari sax section.

What is a destruction device for a flute?

A blowtorch.

How do you get a clarinet out of a tree?

Carve away whatever doesn't look like a clarinet.

What does a bassoon look like to the conductor?

A bazooka.

What do a clarinet and the "Trial of the Century" have in common?

Everyone is relieved when the case is closed.

How do you frustrate a cornet player?

Ask him to sight read.

New at college, Michael wanted to learn more about the music written for heavy metal bands. He headed to the music department office and was referred to one of their well-known professors, Dr. Julliardo. Michael asked, "Can you tell me about heavy metal compositions?" "Of course not," replied Prof. Julliardo. "You need to go to the chemistry department to find someone to help you with that."

Vehicles for Musicians

Allegro Bus

Big Horn Trailer

Canto Bike

Chrysler Royal Airflow

Colt Galant

Hyundai Accent

Isuzu Bellett

Kia Forte

Nissan Rogue

Suzuki Coupe

Morris Minor

How do you get a horn player into the back of a VW Bug?

Grease her hips and leave a Snickers in the back seat.

What is the difference between an oboe and an onion?

Most people cry when they chop up an onion, but almost nobody does when they chop up an oboe.

How can you make a chain saw sound like a baritone sax?
Add some vibrato.

--- //////// ---

What's the difference between a bassoon and a balance beam?
You take your leather boots off before you walk on the balance beam.

--- //////// ---

What is a breath mark?

(a) a dangling comma.

(b) a rising comma.

(c) an apostrophe looking for a word.

(d) an indication you're about to pass out.

(e) a misprint.

Depends on your perspective and how much air you have. It could be any of these.

--- //////// ---

What is the difference between a soprano saxophone and a Harley-Davidson motorcycle?
You can tune a Harley.

--- //////// ---

What does a musician order to eat when he is in a hurry?
Pasta with presto sauce.

--- //////// ---

How do you put down a clarinet?

Call it an oboe.

And how do you put down an oboe?

Call it a clarinet.

What happened when the drummer tried to rejoin the band after his illness?

They balked, due to fear of repercussions.

FRIENDS DON'T LET FRIENDS PLAY DRUMS.

Why are organ players good plumbers?

They know how to open and close all sizes of pipes.

If the music is in "A" and you have a trumpet in "E-flat," where does the trumpet go?

In the case.

How does the music teacher decide which instrument each student should learn?

> He hands each student a clarinet mouthpiece and sees how the student reacts to it. Match them up, based on what student does.

if they...	they learn...
(1) put it in their mouth correctly	(a) Oboe
(2) tap the mouthpiece on the desk	(b) A brass instrument; which one depends on how puffy the student's cheeks are
(3) put it in their mouth horizontally, with the reed down	(c) Flute
(4) put it in pointing down, but with the reed against the upper lip	(d) Singing
(5) blow across the bottom of the mouthpiece	(e) Drums
(6) blow into the bottom of the mouthpiece	(f) Piano
(7) pluck the top of the reed	(g) Saxophone
(8) put it in horizontally and with the reed against the upper lip	(h) Violin

(9) stare at it and tap their fingers on the desk

(i) Assigned to the flag corps if they have good-looking legs or else they go to the softball team

(10) scrape their nails or rub a pencil across the reed

(j) Clarinet

(11) hold the mouthpiece like a microphone

(k) Guitar

(12) toss it across the room

(l) Bassoon

Answers: 1- j, 2—e, 3—g, 4—a, 5—c, 6—b, 7—k, 8—l, 9—f, 10—h, 11—d, 12—i

---

Why are music critics' columns bad choices to line the bottom of a bird cage?

It's too hard to distinguish the droppings from the writings.

What do trumpet players' kids do at the playground?

Try to learn to swing.

And what do trombone players' kids do at the playground?

Try to figure out how to use the slide.

How can you keep your alto sax from being stolen?

Put it in an alto clarinet case.

Sax player to the doctor: Doc, I don't know what's wrong. Some days I feel lousy. I just can't get notes out on my saxophone. My fingers seem uncoordinated. Why is that?

Doctor: How do you feel when you wake up in the morning?

Sax player: Some days I feel like I wake up in a tee-pee and other days in a wigwam.

Doctor: Oh, I know your problem. You're too tense.

Professor Julliardo: Where are bassoons useful besides in bands, woodwind quintets, and orchestras?

Student: Karate classes.

What does a gambler call a soprano sax, an alto sax, a tenor sax, a baritone sax, and a bass sax?

A straight flush.

What would you have if you decided to take all the rock singers in the world and lay them end-to-end across the Sahara Desert?

(a) A good start at a line of Rock-ets.

(b) An offensive line against a camel-mounted force.

(c) A defensive line against rattlesnakes.

(d) A barrier for the build-up of sand dunes.

Depends on why you wanted to do this in the first place.

How do you get A-flat major?

> Swing the trombone around as you march past him and knock him flat onto the ground.

How do you get A-flat minor?

> Roll a bass drum down into the mine.

What is worse than a bagpiper?

> A bagpipe band.

Whom do you hire to clean your band shirt after the concert to get all the spit out of it that drizzled from the trombone player sitting behind you?

> The Irish Washerwoman.

First chair violist: Professor Julliardo, should we play the cello cues?

Professor Julliardo: Sure, go ahead.

First chair cellist to other cellists: They just think they can play this better than we can and want to get better grades than us in orchestra.

A cellist in the second row: That's not why. Violists just like listening to themselves, especially since no one else will listen to them.

What do all drummers need?

Pace-makers, so they can keep a steady beat.

5

Music and Musicians in Nature

Fish

Banded Archerfish

Black Drum Fish

Brassy Chub

Coral Grouper

Diamond Scale Mullet

English Sole

Gopher Rockfish

Guitarfish

Horn Shark

Kelp Rockfish

Longhorn Cowfish

Pickerel

Pipefish

Red Drum Fish

Rockfish

Sea Bass

Sixbar Wrasse

Sole

Starfish

Starry Rockfish

The Bass Band

Which band member can use his instrument to hook fish?
　　The bass flute player.

When your piano sounds awful, who do you call?
　　The Piano Tuna.

Why are fish such good musicians?
　　Because they know all their scales.

Birds

Band-rumped Storm-Petrel

Band-tailed Pigeon

Bar-headed Goose

Bar-tailed Godwit

Bell's Vireo

Clapper Rail

Common Ringed Plover

Great Horned Owl

Hoot Owl

Hornbill

Horned Grebe

Horned Lark

Horned Puffin

Hummingbird

Mute Swan

Piping Plover

Puffin

Reed Bunting

Ring-billed Gull

Ringed Turtle Dove

Ringed Kingfisher

Ringed-neck Pheasant

Ring-necked Duck

Rock Dove

Rock Ptarmigan

Rock Wren

Sandpiper

Scaled Petrel

Scaled Quail

Screech Owl

Sharp-shinned Hawk

Sharp-tailed Grouse

Sharp-tailed Sandpiper

Sharp-tailed Sparrow

Song Sparrow

Trumpeter Swan

Whistling Swan

Whooping Crane

What is a hootenanny?

A group of owls singing and clawing on their banjos.

What do a harp and a chicken have in common?

 They both need plucking.

What do a heron and a string bass have in common?

 A long, straight neck.

What did the band play when a flock of pigeons landed on the lawn in front of their stage at the outdoor summer concert-in-the-park?

 "Up, Up and Away."

Why did the crows suddenly fly off?

 To get away from the fife and drum corps coming across the corn field.

Why were the ducks quacking so loudly?

 They were trying to drown out the bagpipe band.

What's worse than a rooster?

 A bugler who can't tell time.

Amphibians and Reptiles

Banded Rock Lizard

Bell Toad

Cape Horned Lizard

Chorus Frog

Coral Snake

Flat-headed Snake

Flat-tailed Horned Lizard

Flatwoods Salamander

Gopher Snake

Horned Toad

Pygmy Short-horned Lizard

Rattler

Regal Horned Lizard

Ringed Salamander

Ring-necked Snake

Sharp-tailed Snake

Texas Horned Lizard

What is the difference between an electric guitar player and a snake?

> The snake knows when and where to start peeling off.

How is an oboe like a toad?

> Neither one has a neck, they're ugly, they are covered with bumps, and they make strange noises.

Mammals

Big Horn Sheep

Bowhead Whale

Harp Seal

Horned Herefords

Horned Norfolk Cattle

Lipizzaner Horse

Longhorn Cattle

Ringed Seal

Ring-tailed Cat

Ring-tailed Lemur

Rock Rabbit

Rock Squirrel

Rocky Mountain Sheep

Samba Horse

Shorthorn Cattle

Whippet Dog

Whistling Hare

What kind of music can you hear when sitting on the cliffs of Newfoundland?

Harp-seal-chords.

What's the difference between a soprano opera singer and a dolphin?

The dolphin doesn't rupture your eardrums.

What do a contrabass sax and a giant panda have in common?

> Three things: both are the largest of their kind in existence, both are endangered species, and both need cane to function.

Why don't bulls make good music?

> Because their lips aren't long enough to reach their horns.

What's the difference between a pregnant piccolo player and a pregnant manatee (sea cow)?

> About 8 feet and 1,300 pounds, but neither one looks like a mermaid.

What do a contrabass clarinet and a giraffe have in common?

> They both look down on us.

What instrument makes a grizzly sound?

> A bear-i-tone.

What part of a horse do trumpeters like?

> The cornet.

Insects, Spiders

Blow Fly
Bluegrass Billbug
Blues Butterfly
Brassy Ringlet Butterfly
California Ringlet
    Butterfly
Ear Tick
Four-horned Sphinx
    Moth Larva
Hickory-horned Devil
    Moth
Horn Fly
Hornet
Horntail Wasp

Hornworm Moth
Long-Horned Beetle
Plain Ringlet Butterfly
Rose Scale
Scaly-leg Mite
Soft Scale
Spanish Brassy Ringlet
Sticktight Flea
Sweetpotato Hornworm
Swiss Brassy Ringlet
    Butterfly
Tick
Violin Spider
Whirligigs

How to Practice Buzzing

What happens when a bee which thinks he can C-sharp flies into a window?

He becomes a B-flat.

What do flutists and butterflies have in common?

They both can flutter.

What do you call a house occupied by six horn players?

A hornists' nest.

Other Invertebrates, Shells

Belcher's Chorus Shell
Bivalve Mollusk
Coral Rock
European Flat Oyster
Festive Rock Shell
Fiddler Crab
Finger Drupe Shell
Finger Limpet
Flat Periwinkle
Flat Surf Clam
Flattish Horn Shell
Giant Rock Scallop
Glorious Horn Shell
Harp Lora
Harp Shell
Harpa Major Sea Snail
Jingle Shell
Leafy Hornmouth Shell
Lyre Whelk
Ringed Cowry Shell
Ringed Lucina
Rock Barnacles
Rock Borer Mussel
Rock Crab
Rocking Keyhole Limpet
San Diego Ear Shell
Scaly Cockle
Scaly Rock Shell
Triton Trumpet
Trumpet Shell

What is Pearl Jam?

A condiment for your toast that is made from oysters.

What do you call a dozen violists at the bottom of the ocean?

A way to drive deep-sea creatures to the surface.

What are fiddler crabs?

Grumpy members of an Irish band.

What is a crab canon?

The weapon of choice of a ten-legged crustacean.

Animal Band

How do you pay the Animal Band for their services?

With sand dollars.

Repertoire for the Animal Band

Ants Go Marching	Patrick Gilmore
Baby Elephant Walk	Henry Mancini
Bear Symphony	Joseph Haydn
Black Horse Troop	John Philip Sousa
Blackbird	The Beatles
Carnival of Animals	Camille Saint-Saëns
Coral Symphony	Ludwig van Beethoven
Der Alta Brummbár	Julius Fucik
Egotistical Elephant	Don Hartzell
The Firebird	Igor Stravinsky
Flight of the Bumble Bee	Nikolai Rimsky-Korsakov
Frog Legs Rag	James Scott
The Hen and the Cow	George W. Meyer
Horses	Walter Becker and Rickie Lee Jones
Hound Dog	Big Mama Thornton
The Lark Ascending	Vaughan Williams
The Lion King	Elton John and Hans Zimmer
The Little Mermaid	Alan Menken and Howard Ashman
Little Red Rooster	Willie Dixon, arranger of a blues standard
Madame Butterfly	Giacomo Puccini
Peter and the Wolf	Sergei Prokofiev
Pig in a Pen	Traditional bluegrass tune
Pink Panther	Henry Mancini
Pop! Goes the Weasel	English nursery rhyme

Repertoire for the Animal Band (continued)

Puff, the Magic Dragon	Peter Yarrow and Lenny Lipton
Rudolph, the Red-Nosed Reindeer	Johnny Marks
The Spider's Feast	Albert Roussel
Swan Lake	Peter Ilyich Tchaikovsky
The Birds	Andrew David Perkins
The Swan	Camille Saint-Saëns
The Swan of Tuonela	John Sibelius
Three Blind Mice	Thomas Ravenscroft
Tiger Rag	Nick LaRocca
Trout Quintet	Franz Schubert
Turkey in the Straw	David W. Guion
Waltzing Cat	Leroy Anderson
The Whistler and His Dog	Arthur Pryor
White Rabbit	Grace Slick

And, of course, several fox trots.

Paws for Applause

Patricia H. Wheeler

Who should conduct the Animal Band?

> (a) The Whippet Dog.
>
> (b) The Furioso Horse.
>
> (c) The Emperor Penguin.
>
> (d) The Tibetan Terrier.
>
> (e) The Brown-Hooded Cockroach.
>
> (f) The Sharp-Pei.
>
> (g) The Octopus Vulgaris.

Take your pick. Both (c) and (e) are already dressed for the job. And (g) can cue each section of the Animal Band simultaneously! (f) seems pretty sharp. But (a), (b), and (d) all have the temperament of a conductor.

The Penguin Band

Plants for the Musician's Garden

Accent Rose
Angel Trumpet
Ave Maria Rose
Belmont Blue Violas
Blue Bells
Bluegrass
Brass Band Rose
California Poppy
Cobaea Beardtongue
Common Silverbell
Cowhorn Orchid
Crook Neck Squash
Fiddle-leaf Philodendron

Golden Bell Plants
Horn of Plenty Mushrooms
Key-flower Orchid
Mission Bells
Piccolo Tomato Plants
Pipevine
Reba McIntire Rose
Rio Samba Rose
Splendid Violas
Trumpet Honeysuckle
Trombone Squash
Tulips
Windflower

Why did the trumpeter stand on the stump of the freshly-cut pine tree?

He heard he could find perfect pitch there.

What is the favorite kind of music for horses?

Bluegrass.

Rocks, Minerals, and More

Bellatrix
Canis Major
Canis Minor
Capella
Hornblende
Hornfels

Leonis Minorids
Lyra
Trappist
Triangulum
Ursa Major
Ursa Minor

What is the jazziest asteroid in space?

35394 Count-basie, named after one of the greatest jazz musicians of the 20th century.

What is star dust?

Cosmic dust in outer space, some of which falls to Earth. Maybe some of it inspired Hoagy Carmichael to write a song.

What is another name for a rock star?

Asteroid.

Where do lead-headed musicians go?

Into a heavy metal band.

What did the astronaut say to her boss?

"Fly Me to the Moon."

Where do geologists belong?

In a rock band.

Repertoire for the Spacey Rock Band

Across the Universe	John Lennon and Paul McCartney
All of the Stars	Ed Sheeran
All That Is or Ever Was or Ever Will Be	Alan Silvestri
Also Sprach Zarathustra	Richard Strauss
Andromeda	Paul Weller
Aquarius	James Rado and Gerome Ragni
Blue Moon	Richard Rodgers and Lorenz Hart
Deep Field	Eric Whitacre
Fly Me to the Moon	Bart Howard
Here Comes the Sun	George Harrison
Moonlight Sonata	Ludwig van Beethoven
Our Planet	Steven Price
Space Oddity	David Bowie
Stardust	Hoagy Carmichael
The Planets	Gustav Holst
Three Million Light Years From Home	John Williams
Twinkle, Twinkle Little Star	An English lullaby from 1806
Under the Milky Way	Steve Kilbey and Karin Jansson
Walking on the Moon	Gordon Matthew Thomas Sumner (aka Sting)
We All Look to the Stars	Juhi Bansal
When You Wish Upon a Star	Leigh Harline and Ned Washington

6

Jests in Time

Why didn't the guitarist get hired?

He said there were no strings attached.

What did Franz Schubert say when he was asked, "How do you compose?"

"I finish one piece and begin with the next." Then maybe his *Unfinished Symphony* was only supposed to have two movements since he composed much after that.

What mistake did Professor Julliardo make when he planned the marching band's practice?

He forgot to find out when the sprinklers are set to come on.

New band member: Why does the timpanist always start playing when the conductor stops directing?

Long-time band member: So the motion detector won't turn off the lights.

Park Yourself at Our Outdoor Band Concerts

Where can psychiatrists find work?
    In a blues band.

Where do dead-heads belong?
    With the Grateful Dead.

When do alarm clocks go off?
    "In the Wee Small Hours of the Morning."

Ten things the band members can do when Professor Julliardo tells them all to play pianissimo—

 (10) Tell him to go to the back of the auditorium.

 (9) Turn the microphone and speakers off.

 (8) Send him back stage.

 (7) Tell him to stop listening so hard.

 (6) Turn off his hearing aid.

 (5) Put ear muffs on him.

 (4) Put pad savers or mutes in all the wind instruments.

 (3) Stuff cotton in his ears.

 (2) Lean forward and play into the music stands.

 (1) Put their instruments down and quietly hum or whistle their parts, or tap their feet.

What do you do if the fiddler in your Country Western band doesn't show up for the gig?

 Have a cat use the washboard as a scratching post.

What do you call a harmonica player who carries a cell phone?

 Lonely.

Professor Julliardo: Is this a harmonic scale or a natural minor scale?

Student: Neither, it's a symphonic scale.

The Rite of Spring

What do you get if you throw the music critic into the dumpster?

A rotten review.

What has 20 arms and an average IQ of 78?

A ten-piece bagpipe band.

How would you describe a composer with half a brain?

Either analytical or creative.

What do you get if you cross a bugler and a flag pole?

A really stiff bugler.

Patricia H. Wheeler

A man stumbled in late one night, one of many late-night arrivals at home in recent weeks. His wife confronted him and said, "Where were you this time?" "Oh, at the Gold Bar Inn," he mumbled. "Again?" she said. "You were there three other times this week. What is it you like so much about that place?" "Well," he said, "there is gold everywhere—on the tops of the tables, on the chairs, on the coat rack. The glasses are made of gold. Why even the urinal is gold." Not believing a word he said, the wife told her husband to go to bed and get some sleep. Off he stumbled to bed. But she wondered how a place could have so much gold, and if there even really was a Gold Bar Inn. She googled Gold Bar Inn and found its phone number. There it was—the Gold Bar Inn at 555-GOLD. She dialed and got the bartender. Asking him about the gold table tops, he replied, "There are bright specks in the table tops and also on the bar, but they aren't real gold." "And what about the chairs?" "Oh, that is probably the metal wrapped around the base of the legs to protect the wood." "And the coat rack, I suppose you are going to tell me it is made of gold," she said. "Oh no, it's brass," the bartender replied. "Well, certainly the glasses aren't made of gold or brass or any other metal," she commented. "They are glass, but some have yellowed with time and also most of the drinks in them are gold colored, you know, like beer and whiskey." "Right," she said. "I guess my husband is just confused, but one more item he says is gold—the urinal." "Oh my," the bartender declared. He covered the speaker part of the phone and called over to the band. "Hey Barney, I just found out who has been peeing into your baritone saxophone this week." Barney replied, "It would probably help if you posted the restroom sign with the arrow pointing toward the band somewhere else."

What did the trombonist do when the conductor said, "Drop a fifth."?

Grabbed his whiskey bottle and guzzled.

I'll Tune My Horn If You'll Tune Your Engine

What happened when the Army band marched across the battleground while playing a victory march?

The buzzards headed toward the battlefield.

How can flutists increase their practice time?

Blow across empty Coke bottle tops while driving.

And how can sax players increase their practice time?

Suck on straws at the bar.

Some Places for Musicians to Live

Bass Harbor, Maine

Bells, Tennessee

Big Horn, Wyoming

Blue Grass, Iowa

Broken Bow, Oklahoma

Cut Off, Louisiana

Fife, Washington

Greenhorn, Oregon

Key Largo, Florida

Minor, Alabama

Pipestone, Minnesota

Rushing, Arkansas

Sharptown, New Jersey

Toone, Tennessee

What is a C-flute?

A C-piccolo on steroids.

Music teacher: Your daughter played her part with flying colors.

Parent: Oh? What colors were they?

--- —

Why did the band director want the oboe player to sit in the front row?

Because she wore her scherzo high.

--- —

To new members of the Air Force Marching Band, the Director says, "Left, right, left, right, left, right, right, right…" One member asks, "What are we supposed to do, hop on our right leg now?"

--- —

Patient: Will I be able to play string bass after you operate on my hand?

Doctor: Yes, but since I have to cut off a finger, you can only use three strings.

--- —

Late for the performance at the park, Joe, the band's 93-year-old drummer, couldn't find his khaki slacks. But he had his band shirt. When he put his shirt on, he realized that it was long enough to cover his non-percussion equipment. With the good tan on his legs, he thought, "Why not? I'll go this way. No one will notice since I will be behind the bass drum most of the time." Getting to the concert on time, Joe was ready to boom and bang. But part way through the evening, two women in the horn section started giggling. "Did you see Joe's pants tonight? They sure need ironing!"

How did she get her hand stick in her horn?

What do strippers and electric bass players have in common?

They both have G-strings.

What is black and white, and looks good surrounding a conductor?

(a) A pod of killer whales.

(b) 101 Dalmatians.

(c) A flock of emperor penguins.

(d) Musicians in tuxedos.

(e) A family of skunks.

If you are a conductor, probably (d) unless you really like penguins. Otherwise, take your pick.

Student: My mom says some people play piano by ear. Doesn't that hurt their necks and backs?

Music teacher: They have good chiropractors.

What do drummers do during long rests?

Play Pick-Up-Sticks.

What do Tiger Woods and Benny Goodman have in common?

Both are great swingers.

Why is there only one violist in the viola quartet?

There are no parts for the other three violists.

What is an organ grinder?

A butcher who chops liver.

THAT SQUEAKING
IS MY CLARINET,
NOT MY CAR!

Musical Maladies

Mouth Ulcer	Speech Slur
Stiff Neck	Club Foot
Headache	Tympanoplasty
Tongue Glossitis	Arrhythmia
Mitral Valve Prolapse	Staph Infection
Ruptured Ear Drum	Poor Balance
Muscle Strain	Labored Breathing
Cleft Lip	Broken Bones

Why did the tuba player stand on the stool?

He was trying to reach the high notes.

What kind of music is like a foreign language?

Latin.

Why do kids want to learn to play drums?

> (a) They like to hit things and not get in trouble.
>
> (b) Their parents won't let them practice at home.
>
> (c) They feel like they're on a power trip if the band follows their beat rather than the conductor's baton.
>
> (d) They don't have to carry their instrument home from school each day.

I don't know. Ask them if they haven't lost their hearing yet.

What is a bass flute?

> An over-weight C-flute that took a wrong turn.

What do you call a trumpet player who carries a pager?

> An optimist.

What do John Philip Sousa and Michael Jackson have in common?

> Both wear white gloves.

Why are timpanists like lightning?

> They rarely strike the same spot more than once.

Patricia H. Wheeler

Some Vehicles for Musicians

American Motors Hornet

Chevy Bel Air

Fiat 500 Pop

Heartland Bighorn Trailer

Kia Cadenza

Monteverdi High Speed

Nissan Altima

Optare Tempo Bus

Rolls Royce

Wolseley Hornet

7

Good Last Names
for Musicians

(See Chapter 2 for more)

𝄢

Last Names for Brass Players

Blower	Spitz
Brass	Strayhorn
Bugler	Trebelhorn
Einhorn	Trombino
Flugel	Trumpeter
Hornblower	VanHorn
Lowhorn	

Patricia H. Wheeler

Last Names for Percussionists

Banger   Mallet

Boomer   Ringer

Chime   Rumble

Clapper   Sticker

Ding   Tamberino

Dingle   Tingle

Drummer   Trapps

Gong

Last Names for String Players

Bowman   Plucker

Fiddler   Stringfellow

Harpman   Strum

LeBow   Violante

Luter   Violinsky

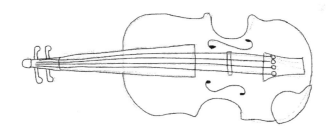

Last Names for Woodwind Players

Airey

Basson

Fife

Fluter

Flutter

Lipper

Piciulo

Reedman

Reedy

Saxer

Saxman

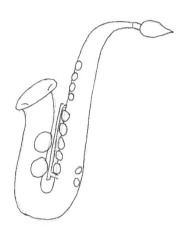

Last Names for Singers

Alto

Altobello

Bass

Cantor

Carol

Heartsong

Hummer

Sangmaster

Singer

Songster

Sung

Tenorio

Tsang

Voyce

Wysinger

Patricia H. Wheeler

Last Names for Composers

Allegro	Major
Bar	Minor
Fortissimo	Mixer
Fine	Presto
Flat	Rest
Harmony	Scales
Key	Sharp
Kleffman	Treble
Koral	Trillo
Largoza	Triplett

Last Names for Conductors

Baton	Pitch
Beat	Record
Counts	Stickler
Maestri	Stickrod
Mix	Tone
Pae	Tune
Pickup	

Last Names of Music Genres

Arias	Operaio
Band	Organ
Blue	Ragland
Chamber	Rapp
Dixie	Rock
Duett	Rondo
Jazz	Soloman
Koral	Suite
Latin	Swing
March	Tango
Medley	Waltz

Patricia H. Wheeler

8

Major Giggles

mf

Conductor: We've played this piece so many times over the years. How can you forget the key changes?

Piccolo player: But we're older now.

What do you call a cymbal player in a three-piece suit?

The defendant.

Maple Leaf Rag Dancing Duo

Murphy's Laws for Musicians—

When you finally have a really good reed, you slice it when putting your mouth cap on.

When you are ready for your timpani solo, the bass drummer always has one of your sticks.

When you are not feeling good and are playing at an outdoor concert, the turkey vultures hover overhead.

When you're playing at the concert, you discover that you have the wrong arrangement of a piece in your folder.

When it's a windy day at your outdoor gig, you discover that your wife took the clothes pins out of your gig bag so she could hang up the laundry outside for the solar dryer.

When you smile at the audience during your solo, it messes up your embouchure.

When you arrive at rehearsal, you realize you have the folder for another band.

When you pick up your C-piccolo and start to play, you realize that you are looking at a D-flat piccolo part.

When you start to put your trombone together, you find that you have your trumpet mouthpiece in your trombone case instead.

What kind of music do physicists study?

Fusion.

What kind of music do they play in Heaven?

Soul.

Some Vehicles for Musicians

Anthem Trailer

Chrysler Airflow

Ferrari Superfast

Hyundai Chorus Bus

Kia Soul Plus

Mazda Protege

Nissan Stanza

Porsche Speedster

Sing (Chinese car model)

Ford Fusion

What do you call hard-of-hearing sound engineers?

    (a) De Blaster.

    (b) Da Big Amp.

    (c) Von Blair.

    (d) El Fortissimo.

    (e) Sir Blasting.

Depends on what damage is done to their ears! Might be a ruptured eardrum.

What do athletes, botanists, musicians, and physicists study?

    Pitch.

What do trombone players and plumbers both have in their kits?

    Tubing and plungers.

What do workaholic trumpeters do on their days off?

    Practice *Bugler's Holiday*.

What did Chuck Berry say when he got home from his road trip?

    "Too Pooped to Pop!"

During the Christmas concert, the conductor wanted to have a sing-along with the audience on some carols, so he had some musicians in the band sing instead of play. When one of the clarinet players was asked to sing, she said, "Why do you think I took clarinet lessons? Because I couldn't sing!"

What did the agent say to the guitarist who wanted to join the band?

"So You Want To Be A Rock 'n' Roll Star"?

Who enrolled in Professor Julliardo's music class?

The Four Freshmen.

Which band do you want when a stranger is *Walking In Your Footsteps*?

The Police.

Professor Julliardo: What method do bassoonists use to get the fluid out of their butt joints?

Student: Spinal Tap.

What Happens When Drummers Eat Greasy
Drumsticks and Fries Before Rehearsal?

What did the soprano say to the bass?

You have your music upside down.

Who takes kids to concerts?

The Mamas and the Papas.

Why were students upset with Professor Julliardo's lecture?

They thought Music Appreciation meant they
would be listening to music.

How do frustrated composers destroy their pianos?

There's the Hammer-Stein-way and the Bern-Stein-Way.

Top eight ways for musicians to make money—

(8) Dumpster diving for aluminum cans so they can use pull tabs for guitar picks.

(7) Using the washboard to do laundry while making music.

(6) Selling ear plugs to the neighbors of their rock 'n roll friends.

(5) Checking coin return boxes on pay phones, while they still take coins.

(4) Being a street musician near the train station.

(3) Cleaning windshields at stop lights.

(2) Playing on their balcony during the Coronavirus and tossing out self-addressed envelopes asking for tips.

(1) Sanitizing other musicians instruments.

What kind of musicians sometimes play on the edge?

Timpanists.

What do accordion players use as birth control?

Their personalities.

What should you do when the conductor is up to his neck in quicksand?

Get more quicksand, quickly.

What does Professor Julliardo want for Christmas?

Twelve chimers clanging

Eleven carolers caroling

Ten handbell players ringing

Nine clarinetists chirping

Eight flutists tooting

Seven trumpeters blaring

Six trombonists blasting

Five drummers drumming

Four hornists blurting

Three oboists squawking

Two tubists booming

And one large, happy audience

I LIKE TO CONDUCT
TRAFFIC AND BANDS

Patricia H. Wheeler

What does the sign on the music professor's door say?

Bach in forte minuets.

What music goes with burgers and fries?

Pop.

What is the difference between a cemetery and a viola recital?

People are dying to get into the cemetery and dying to get out of the viola recital.

When can too high a pitch be life-threatening?

When you are a roofer.

Tommy: Why do they call it the *Pathetic Symphony*?
Bobby: I don't know. I didn't think it was so bad.

What do Bill Clinton and Miles Davis have in common?

Both like to toot their own horns.

Professor Julliardo: What is a requiem?
Student: The course we had to take before this one.

Following a band concert at the nursing home, one of the residents came up and said, "When I was your age, I played an instrument too. It took lots of time to tune it just right. I could play all kinds of music on it—jazz, big band, classical." A young member of the band then asked him, "Oh really, what instrument did you play?" The resident replied, "The radio."

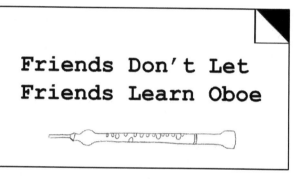

Friends Don't Let Friends Learn Oboe

Whom does the piano player hope to get a call from?

The owner of the local bar.

What's the different between a French horn and an English horn?

You can catch a ball in the French horn.

What kind of personality do timpanists have?

A headstrong one.

Some Places for Musicians to Live

Baton Rouge, Louisiana

Belltown, Delaware

Bluebell, Utah

Canon City, Colorado

Dixie, Georgia

Fife Lake, Michigan

Harmony, Rhode Island

Mixville, Connecticut

Poorman, Alaska

Rising Star, Texas

Rockingham, Vermont

Rushville, Nebraska

Show Low, Arizona

Trap, North Carolina

What did the efficiency expert say to the orchestra board in his report?

(1) You have all these people playing the same part. You only need one first violin, one second violin, one viola, etc.

(2) Cut out all the rests in the brass parts. Just have them play through their parts and leave early so you don't have to pay them as much.

(3) Get rid of the conductor. Nobody is watching him.

How do you get people to dislike you?

Toot your own horn too much.

If an oboe is a licorice stick, what is a bassoon?

A red vines candy.

What kind of background music should you play at the bar?

Music that drives people to drink.

The band arrived at Walnut High School to play at their spring dance. Eric had set his bass guitar, leaning against the amp at the back corner of the stage. Jason, the drummer, let Eric know that one of the kids came up behind his bass and played with one of the pegs. Eric asked Jason which peg it was. Jason said, "I don't know. Why does that matter?" Eric replied, "I need to know which peg it was so I know which string is out of tune."

9

Student Excuses for Not Practicing

Treble—What students who don't practice get into!

My father used my baritone mouthpiece for a funnel to put gasoline in the lawn mower.

I lost my ligature and I couldn't find a rubber band that worked.

I sliced my reed when I put the cap back on my mouthpiece.

My swab got stuck in my sax.

My little brother sat on my flute and turned it into a boomerang.

My dad used my drum sticks to hold up the tomato plants.

I picked up my sax by its neck and...well, I know you warned me, but....

My mom is pregnant and when I practice, she gets nauseous.

I ran out of reeds and forgot to ask my dad to buy a new box for me.

I can't practice drums until my little sister finishes her homework, but I can't practice after my dad gets home from work, and my sister took too long to do her homework.

My eyes are too tired. I had to take a long multiple-choice test today.

I had to use my practice time to write down some jokes before I forgot them.

Well, you told me to work on #23, but I didn't know if you meant exercise 23 or page 23, so I watched Michael Jordan instead.

I've been too Bizet, Bizet, Bizet and, at times, I get Liszt-less.

I ate too much pizza.

My trombone slide slid to the bottom of the pool when I tried to clean it.

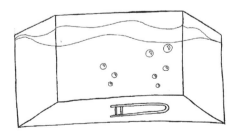

Patricia H. Wheeler

A wad of gum got stuck in my mouthpiece.

My instrument was recalled by the factory because it could backfire.

The police took my instrument because I was disturbing the peace.

My mom made me watch MTV with her.

I forgot to pick up my instrument at the repair shop.

Don't try using any of these unless you have confirming evidence that it is true in your case, and don't get any ideas for excuses either. Remember, if you want to get to Carnegie Hall, you must practice.

10

Comical Measures

What is the difference between the dead piccolo player in the road and the dead flutist in the road?

The skid marks in front of the flutist.

___

Why was the bass drummer kicked out of the band?

He missed a beat.

___

What happens to musicians who can't afford to buy any clothes?

Ragtime.

___

What do you call a drunk musician after he drinks a bottle of bourbon?

A diminished fifth.

___

How do musicians find food at night?

Pull the Handel on the refrigerator.

A visitor at a Native American village was impressed by the continuous drumming at their pow-wow—day and night, day after day, but found she wasn't getting enough sleep. She asked one of the tribal leaders, "When does the drumming stop?" The leader, very somber, answered, "Drums not stop, very bad." Still short on sleep, the visitor inquired again the next day, asking the leader, "Exactly what do you mean by 'very bad?'" The chief then stepped forward and said, "When drums stop, bass solo starts. Very bad."

Why don't people go to the movies as much as they use to?

They are tired of all the sax and violins.

Why does the drummer have a fax machine in his car?

Every time he passes a nightclub, he faxes them his resume.

Why did the musicians' union ask the organist to be their negotiator with management?

> Because she knows when to pull out the stops.

Why are drummers' lungs coveted for transplants?

> Because they hold a lot of air and have had little use.

Eleven ways to know if someone is in a handbell choir—

(11) They turn to the nearest church at noon each day.

(10) They like to walk around town ringing doorbells.

(9) They have clocks throughout their home that play Westminster Chimes every 15 minutes.

(8) They ring the bell at the checkout counter, even if the cashier is there.

(7) They like to go out the emergency exits and set off fire alarm bells.

(6) They shake everything they pick up.

(5) They always wear gloves.

(4) They frequently complain of carpal tunnel syndrome from their musical pastime.

(3) They like to be with groups of dingy people.

(2) They are usually waiting for someone else to take action.

(1) They arrive at class just after the bell rings.

Patricia H. Wheeler

Why are bassoonists so fat?

Because all the water collects in their butts.

Why do jazz bands play *When the Saints Go Marching In* so often?

To remind their audience to behave themselves, even if they are having a good time.

Heaven's Band

Professor Julliardo: Why do we usually tune our instruments to the oboe?

Student: Because the oboist doesn't know how to tune his own instrument.

Have you ever noticed how old instruments keep showing up again? Remember that old clarinet you had in high school, and you let your children learn to play on it? Then they went off to better clarinets or other instruments and stuck yours back in the closet. When it came time for the grandchildren to learn an instrument, out came that clarinet again. And each of your grandchildren returned it to the same closet after getting started and then moving on to other and better instruments. Old clarinets just seem to know where home is; if only they knew how to stay in tune as well.

Hell's Band

What was the Battle of the Little Bighorn?

A competition between tenor tuba players.

Patricia H. Wheeler

How are a hunter and a glockenspiel player in the marching band alike?

> They both must be able to accurately hit moving targets.

———

How do you get a clarinetist down from a tree?

> You could cut the noose, but leave him there unless you really are desperate for clarinet players.

———

Was John Philip Sousa born in March?

> Of course not. He wasn't the March King at birth. But the March King did march into heaven in March of 1932.

———

What problem do many guitar players have?

> They are too strung out.

———

What musician has a beautiful lady on his arm?

> The string bass player. It's a tattoo.

———

Professor Julliardo: Do you play better now that you had your horn repaired?

Student: No, but the horn plays better.

———

Why is it dangerous to sit in front of the row of horns?

> If they all dump at once, you can be hit by a tidal wave.

What do musicians enter after a late-night performance?

> The twilight zone.

Some Vehicles for Musicians

Blast Trailer

Chrysler Concorde

Ford Tempo

Hummer

Jazz Trailer

Mazda Bongo

Nissan Figaro

Opel Rekord

Piper Cub

Patricia H. Wheeler

What is the dynamic range of—

a trombone	IN and OUT
an electric bass	ON and OFF
a triangle	DING and…silence…
a trumpet	BLARE and BLURT
a clarinet	SQUEAK and MOAN
a horn	HONK and BACKFIRE
castanets	CLICK and CLACK
a drum	RATTLE and ROLL
a piccolo	HIGH and VERY HIGH
a string bass	LOW and VERY LOW
a violin	PULSATE and THROB
a piano	PING and PONG
a viola	SCREECH and HOWL
a tuba	GROAN and GRUNT
a saxophone	SQUEAK and WAIL
a tambourine	JINGLE and JANGLE
an oboe	IMPLODE and EXPLODE
timpani	RUMBLE and BOOM
cymbals	BANG and BRUSH
a harp	PLUCK and PLUNG
a guitar	STRUM and PICK
a bagpipe	QUACK and SQUAWK
a cello	BACK and FORTH
a harmonica	RIGHT and LEFT
an accordion	EXPAND and CONTRACT
chimes	CLING and CLANG
a flute	TWEET and CHIRP
a bassoon	It has no dynamics.

Why are banjo players' brains in demand for transplants?

Who said they are?

Why do tuba players wear diapers?

To catch all the moisture that drips from their horns.

Bill: Why on earth did you start learning how to play bag-pipes?

Bruce: I heard it was a non-toxic way to get cockroaches out of the house.

Bill: Maybe so, but it sure isn't an environmentally friendly way to do it!

Professor Julliardo: What is a wind symphony?

Student: Depends on how fast they are playing. Could be anything from a gentle breeze to a tornado.

What do musicians do for exercise?

Bee-bop, hip-hop, rock, and swing.

**If You Want To Duet Better,
Quit And Hire Two Musicians**

Some Places for Musicians to Live

Beatty, Nevada

Benbow, California

Bow, New Hampshire

Brilliant, Alabama

Canon, Georgia

Dixie Valley, Nevada

Flat, Alaska

Harmony Hill, Delaware

La Belle, Missouri

Ragland, Kentucky

Rock, Massachusetts

Saxeville, Wisconsin

Singer, Louisiana

Triangle, New York

Woods Bay, Montana

What do you call an accordion player who carries a beeper?

Desperate for work.

What's the difference between an extra-large pizza and a musician?

The pizza can feed a family of six.

What's the difference between a trumpet and a rocket?

A couple decibels.

Who likes to play solos on their balcony?

People sheltering-at-home during the COVID-19 pandemic.

Why is a string bass like your grandparents?

You need help getting them in and out of the car.

While tuning up before rehearsal, Toni said to the two flute players next to her, "You are out of tune. My flute teacher told me to tune to 438 because then I would sound brighter." Stacie told Toni, "The band tunes to 440." Toni objected and continued tuning her flute to 438 and insisting that the rest of the band was out of tune.

11

Knock, Knock Jokes

Who do you call when all those Knock-Knockers have knocked down your door?

> The Carpenters?

> The Rappers?

> The Police?

Knock, knock.
Who's there?
Vanna.
Vanna who?
Vanna you going to join our band?

Knock, knock.
Who's there?
Gonna.
Gonna who?
Gonna play a love song for you on my accordion.

Knock, knock.
Who's there?
Wda.
Wda who?
Wda pair of banjo players in your house.

Knock, knock.
Who's there?
Ima.
Ima who?
Ima gonna sell you some candy bars so I can get my horn
   repaired.

Knock, knock.
Who's there?
Mari.
Mari who?
Mariachi band to entertain you during your dinner of
   burritos and tacos.

Knock, knock.
Who's there?
Picka.
Picka who?
Picka-low Pete to play *The Stars and Stripes Forever* for you.

Knock, knock.
Who's there?
Isabel.
Isabel who?
Isabel player at home? We need one more in the bell
  choir.

Knock, knock.
Who's there?
Hank.
Hank who?
Hank you for not playing your viola this evening.

Knock, knock.
Who's there?
Harry.
Harry who?
Harry up and come to our gig.

Knock, knock.
Who's there?
Data.
Data who?
Data way to play your trumpet—muted!

Knock, knock.
Who's there?
Andy.
Andy who?
Andy sat on his violin.

Knock, knock.
Who's there?
Juicy.
Juicy who?
Juicy our band in the parade?

Knock, knock.
Who's there?
Tuna.
Tuna who?
Piano tuna sent by your neighbors.

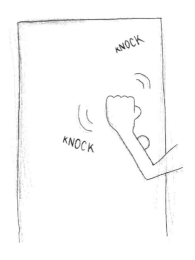

Knock, knock.
Who's there?
My Nirvana.
My Nirvana who?
My Nirvana edge when you practice your drum set.

Patricia H. Wheeler

Knock, knock.
Who's there?
Strum.
Strum who?
Strum-ming on my banjo for you.

Knock, knock.
Who's there?
Hum.
Hum who?
Hum-ming your favorite tune.

Knock, knock.
Who's there?
Suzu.
Suzu who?
Suzu-ki, holder of the key to your violin case.

Knock, knock.
Who's there?
Verdi.
Verdi who?
Verdi concert tonight?

Knock, knock.
Who's there.
Con.
Con who?
Concerto for Viola recordings for sale. Want to buy
    some?

Knock, knock.
Who's there?
Bangem.
Bangem who?
Bangem, the drummer you whistled at in the parade.

Knock, knock.
Who's there?
Fiddle.
Fiddle who?
Fiddle-ling around today; nothing better to do.

Knock, knock.
Who's there?
Harmon.
Harmon who?
Harmon, your favorite harmonica player.

Knock, knock.
Who's there?
Flutie.
Flutie who?
Flutie Tutti. Whootie else?

Knock, knock.
Who's there?
Kazoo.
Kazoo who?
Kazoo take me to band rehearsal tonight?

Patricia H. Wheeler

Knock, knock.
Who's there?
Bea.
Bea who?
Bea-ware of the bagpipe band headed this way.

Knock, knock.
Who's there?
Tim.
Tim who?
Tim Pani, the poor musician collecting canned goods.

Knock, knock.
Who's there?
Tuba.
Tuba who?
Tuba toothpaste you wanted to borrow.

Knock, knock.
Who's there?
Telemann.
Telemann who?
Telemann I'm looking for a violist to play my concerto.

Knock, knock.
Who's there?
Juli.
Juli who?
Julliardo, your Professor, to see if you are practicing.

Knock, knock.
Who's there?
Man.
Man who?
Man-dolin me some lute and a guitar?

Knock, knock.
Who's there?
Vera.
Vera who?
Vera good accordion player to entertain you.

Knock, knock.
Who's there?
Iris.
Iris who?
Iris my ears when your punk rock band stops making
   noise.

Knock, knock.
Who's there?
Emma Lou.
Emma Lou who?
Emma Lou-zing money being a musician, so I'm mowing
lawns. Can I do yours for ten bucks?

Knock, knock.
Who's there?
Juana.
Juana who?
Juana go to the jazz festival with me?

Ring, ring.
Ring, ring.
Knock, knock.
Pound, pound.
Who's there.
Jus.
Jus who?
Jus wanted to see if you can hear the doorbell while
you're practicing drums.

Knock, knock.
Who's there?
Your sonata….
My sonata? I don't have a sonata!
You know, your 14-year-old son, Otto.
Oh, him.
Your son-ata practice his horn when your neighbors
aren't trying to sleep.

Knock, knock.
Who's there?
D Major.
D Major who?
D Major with the Army band to find out why you weren't
at marching practice this afternoon.

Knock, knock.
Who's there?
John Lennon.
John Lennon? Aren't you dead?
John Lennon you his boom box.

Knock, knock.
Who's there?
Wynonna.
Wynonna who?
Wynonna there to answer the door when you're
practicing viola.

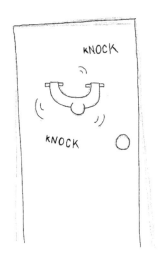

Patricia H. Wheeler

Knock, knock.
Who's there?
Huey Lewis and the News.
The Huey Lewis and the News? Wow!
No wow, Huey Lewis and the newspaper carrier to collect our fees.

Knock, knock.
Who's there?
Mrs. Anderson Anderson.
Huh? Am I hearing double?
No, no.
An echo?
Nope. It's Mrs. Anderson Anderson, Leroy, to take you for a Sleigh Ride.

Knock, knock.
Who's there?
Sonny Rollins.
Sonny Rollins? Really?
Your Sonny Rollins down the hill towards a brick wall.

Knock, knock.
Who's there?
Oboist.
Oboist who?
This oboist looking for a hot meal and a place to sleep.
I missed the freight train.

Knock, knock.
Who's there?
Philharmonic.
Philharmonic who?
Your tree is philharmonic butterflies.

Knock, knock.
Who's there?
Lawrence Welk.
The Lawrence Welk? Where are the bubbles?
Here in the champagne bottle. Lawrence Welk welk-comes
   you to the neighborhood

Knock, knock.
Who's there?
Jute.
Jute who?
Jute box ready for your quarters.

Knock, knock.
Who's there?
Bassoon.
Bassoon who?
Bassoon or later the tax collector will catch up with you.

Knock, knock.
Who's there?
Tuba.
Tuba who?
Tuba or not tuba a musician. Can't decide.

Patricia H. Wheeler

Knock, knock.
Who's there?
Aida.
Aida who?
Aida the pizza before it got cold.

Knock, knock.
Who's there?
Accordion.
Accordion who?
Accordion to the IRS you are five years behind in taxes.

12

Whimsical Music

♭

What do lonely musicians like to do in their off-time?
Bizet Bartók at the local pub.

— —

How do poor musicians get from one city to the next?
"Take the A Train" or, if they miss that, hop onto
the Coltrane.

— —

How do rich musicians get from one city to the next?
Fly first class on the Jefferson Airplane.

— —

What is black and brown, and looks good on a conductor?
A Doberman.

— —

A sleepy accordion player tried driving straight through the night to get to his gig, but had to stop at a roadside cafe for a cup of coffee. As the caffeine kicked in, he realized that he hadn't locked his car and had left his accordion in the back seat. Rushing back out to the parking lot, he discovered it was too late—someone had already gotten into his car. Now there were two more accordions in the back seat plus one in front and two on the roof rack.

What do you get if you cross a horn player and a goal post?

A horn player with a bump on her head.

How can you make a tubist play staccato?

Put a tenuto mark over a whole note and mark it "solo."

metro gnome

How is a soprano sax similar to a ballistic missile?

They are offensive and inaccurate.

What is the first test in Round One of the World Bassoon Competition?

Assemble the bassoon without looking at the directions.

How are an electronic tuner and a vacuum cleaner the same?

When you turn them on, they suck.

Student: Who is Jacques Ibert?

Professor Julliardo: Well, I can assure you that he isn't related to Yogi Bear.

Patricia H. Wheeler

What do musicians call a rock slide?

    (a) Chapter 11 bankruptcy.

    (b) The Rolling Stones.

    (c) The down side of manic-depression.

    (d) The trombone in the Rock Band.

    Take your pick. They're all rock slides.

What is the difference between a conductor and the PLO?

    You can negotiate with the PLO.

What do you call a horn player who is wandering the streets?

    Strayhorn.

What did the sophomore percussion student do when Professor Julliardo told him to practice his roll?

    Strapped the bass drum to a skate board and sent it downhill.

A conductor has two kidneys, but we can't use either one for a transplant. Why not?

    Conductors have a lot of waste to process after each rehearsal and need both kidneys.

Some Places for Musicians to Live

Bell, California

Big Bone, Kentucky

Bow Valley, Nebraska

Carol City, Florida

Drum Point, Maryland

Flat Lick, Kentucky

Harpers Ferry, West Virginia

New Harmony, Utah

Organ, New Mexico

Rock Camp, Ohio

Rockville, Connecticut

Sharp, Texas

Triplet, Virginia

Woodstown, New Jersey

Why couldn't Mozart find his teacher?

Because he was Haydn.

Patricia H. Wheeler

What is the difference between a percussionist and a drummer?

The rudiments.

What is kept in conductors' files?

Scores and scores of scores.

What is the difference between a classical flutist and a jazz flutist?

For one, the moisture in the flute is condensation and for the other, it's drizzle.

What's the difference between a French horn player and a harmonica player?

The harmonica player is supposed to suck when he plays.

Say you're in a room with a serial killer, a terrorist leader, and a conductor, and you have a gun with only two bullets. What should you do?

Shoot the conductor twice.

Top ten reasons for firing your band's conductor:

(10) He doesn't know how to find his way to the podium.

(9) He falls off the stage when he steps back off the podium.

(8) His toupee keeps falling off whenever he takes a bow.

(7) He keeps looking at the legs of the female musicians in the front row.

(6) He refuses to wear tails.

(5) He doesn't know the score.

(4) He doesn't know how to count.

(3) He keeps trying to conduct with a twirling baton.

(2) He thinks a conductor's job is to collect tickets.

(1) He thinks he is the great Professor Julliardo.

What was the tuba player's favorite song from *The Wizard of Oz*?

"If I Only Had a Brain."

If there are a conductor and a moose lying in the road ahead, which one should you run over?

> The conductor—you might get paid for finishing the job.

We took up a collection for our band director's funeral, asking for $50 from community leaders. One of them sent us $100 with a note to bury two conductors.

Student: Why does a fermata mark look like an eye peering over the notes?

Music Teacher: To remind you to look up at the conductor.

How do you know your dentist doesn't want to clean your teeth?

Because he's sitting in his office picking on his banjo while you sit in the waiting room.

What three talents does every band want from their percussionists?

They can (1) count, (2) follow the conductor, and (3) play drums.

The musician, recently accepted into Heaven by Saint Peter, was greeted by an angel. "You'll be assigned to the Heavenly Band, of course," said the angel, as she pointed to the instrument room. Delighted, the musician picked up his new instrument and headed for the band room. The angel said, "One word of caution. It's a great band, but God has this girlfriend who thinks she's a great singer...."

What is the difference between a conductor and a snare drummer?

One stick.

What composer did his best to foster independence for himself?

Stephen Foster, born on the Fourth of July, 1826.

How do you shut up an electric bass player?

Pull the plug on the amp.

Patricia H. Wheeler

What are the critical items for an instrument repair technician's kit?

Duct tape, all-purpose glue, straight pins, paper clips, cotton balls, Q-tips, drain cleaner, plunger, rags, hammers, wire coat hangers, clothes pins, needle and thread, safety pins, and plastic garbage bags for all the extra instrument parts.

Student: Why do we call a recorder a recorder when it doesn't record anything?

Music Teacher: Hmm, let me get back to you on that one.

Who was the better composer, Mozart or Moses?

Moses—he had the superior staff.

Clarinetist: Why does anyone want to learn to play oboe? It is so nasal-sounding and unpleasant.

Flutist: Why would anyone keep playing oboe? It sounds the same way 20 years later!

Singer: Next time I sing that song with you, can I modulate from the key of D minor to the key of G major the second time?

Guitar player: Why do you ask? You have been doing that already.

Some Vehicles for Musicians

Chevrolet Beat
Ford Freestyle
Honda Accord
Mazda Carol
Nissan Leaf
Pontiac GT Vibe
Reed Boat

Rumba Tandem Bicycle

13

How Many Musicians Does It Take to Change a Lightbulb?

Piccolo players	Only one, but you will have to replace all the lightbulbs that shattered while she was practicing *The Stars and Stripes Forever*.
Flutists	Just one, but the flutist will spend $10,000.00 on a shiny, sterling silver bulb.
Oboists	Only one, but by the time he is done shaving the tip, you will need a new bulb.
English horn players	One, but she falls off the ladder while trying to line it up just right.

Bassoonists	Two, one to set the bulb in the top of the bassoon and one to turn the bassoon, but note that they only change ceiling lights.

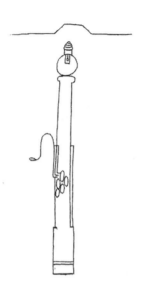

E-flat clarinet players	Just one, but the bulbs always squeak when they change them.
Clarinetists	One, but she will go through a whole box of bulbs to find one that doesn't squeak when she blows on it.
Alto clarinet players	One, and he will do an excellent job if you provide him with detailed instructions.
Bass clarinet players	One, but she will squawk about the job incessantly.

Patricia H. Wheeler

Soprano sax players	Two, one to change the bulb and one to compile jokes about how the other musicians are changing lightbulbs.
Alto sax players	Five, one to change the lightbulb and four to tell him he used the wrong kind of bulb.
Tenor sax players	One, but he will spend time going through all the lightbulbs to find the one that gives off the smoothest lighting.
Bari sax players	Two, one to put in the new bulb and one to "bari" the old bulb.
Bass sax players	One, but it must be near the floor because they like doing low-down jobs.
Horn players	Two, one for the bulb and one to keep the first player from putting her hand in the socket.
Cornet players	Two, one to hold the bulb and the other to drink until the room spins.
Trumpet players	Five, one to change the bulb and the other four to brag about how much higher they could reach.
Buglers	One, but he does it so loudly that he wakes up everybody else.
Trombone players	One, but she will slide it in, so only give her long fluorescent bulbs to change.

Bass trombone players	One, but he is going to customize the switch too.
Baritone players	Five, so they can vote on which clef to use for each bulb.
Tuba players	One, but he keeps looking for a bigger bulb.
Sousaphone players	Just one, but have lots of lightbulbs on hand because he keeps dropping them into his horn hoping they will brighten up his playing.
String bass players	None. The piano player will change it for him with her left hand.
Electric guitar players	Two, but they stand so close to each other you'd swear they were going to kiss.
Electric bass players	One, but he will do it so loudly that the bulb shatters.
Banjo players	Don't ask them to do it because they will keep plucking at the bulbs until they are all broken.
Drummers	Once the bulb is inserted, they hit it with a stick and it breaks and needs another replacement. A never-ending job for drummers.

Patricia H. Wheeler

Cymbal players	Just one, and she can change several bulbs during the 64-bar rest.
Timpani players	Four, each with a different size lightbulb, and they will need time to decide which size bulb to use in each socket.
Bell ringers	One, but she will shake it to see if it has a good clapper.
Pianists	Don't ask her. She is already busy changing the lightbulb for the string bass player.
Fiddlers	He'll be fiddling around so much he will never get it done.
Violists	Don't know. First you have to tell them what a lightbulb is.
Cellists	One, but he will hold it between his knees and try to turn the bulb, leading to pulled back muscles and a broken lightbulb (unless he is also a gymnast).
Accordion players	Two, one to read the directions while the other tries to change the bulb.
Bagpipers	One, but he might crush the bulb under his arm.

Organists	One, but she will play a hymn first asking God for protection from electrocution.
Harmonica players	One, but he won't screw it in. He will stick it up with duct tape.
Conductors	One, because he just holds it and the world revolves around him.
Associate conductors	We don't know as nobody ever watches him.
Music teachers	Just one, but nobody is watching.
Drum majors	Two, one to install the bulb and one to catch it when he turns it the wrong way.
Band managers	One, but she will call the musicians on her list and get one of them to do it for her.
Instrument repairers	One, but he will fine tune and adjust the entire lighting fixture first.
Soloists	Always one. Soloists never share the spotlight.

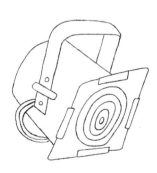

Patricia H. Wheeler

Chorus members	Five, one to hold the bulb and the others to turn her around and around.
Opera singers	None, because their agents do it.
Country Western singers	Three, one to change the lightbulb and two to write a song about the burned-out lightbulb they miss now.
Heavy Metal band	The entire band and they will do it so loudly the ceiling might come down.
Bluegrass musicians	Three, one to change it and two to complain that it's electric.
Bass singers	Don't ask them to do ceiling lights. They can't get up that high.
Music critics	Don't ask them. They don't know how to change a lightbulb. But they will find something wrong with the way everyone else does it.
Sound crew	One, but he will do lots of testing… testing…testing.

Union stagehands	Thirty-two. You gotta problem with that?
Ushers	One, but he can't figure out where to put it.
Lighting crew	None. They like working in the dark.
Board members	Six. They can't do anything without a quorum.
Band boosters	Several. They will form a committee to write procedures and then appoint a band member or section to do it.
Jr. high band students	Four, one to change the bulb while three sit back and huff, "I could do a better job than that."

14

Quasi Quips

ppp

What is the difference between a baritone and a tuba?

The time needed for melt-down.

How do you make a trombone sound like a horn?

Stick your hand in the bell and play a lot of wrong notes.

And how do you make a horn sound like a trombone?

Pull out all the slides and play out of tune.

How much does a good conductor weigh?

About four pounds, not counting the urn.

How are a trombone and a chain saw alike?

If the person holding either of them turns too quickly, he can cut off somebody's head.

Saint Peter was checking in new arrivals at the Pearly Gate. The newly revised procedures called for assigning places in Heaven by the applicant's last Earthly salary. He asked the first person in line, "How much did you make last year?" The person replied, "Two-hundred thousand before taxes." The gatekeeper said, "Oh, a doctor! Welcome!" When the next person in line was asked the same questions, he responded, "Eighteen thousand," to which Peter replied, "Cool. What instrument do you play?"

What is the difference between a bass drum and a trampoline?

You take your shoes off before jumping on the trampoline.

What is the difference between a tenor drum and a bass drum?

It takes longer to crush the bass drum.

What is the difference between a snare drum and a bass drum?

The bass drum has no snare.

How do you turn a straight soprano sax into a curved soprano sax?

Run a rototiller over it.

What does a timpanist say when he gets to the gig?

"Would you like fries with that, sir?"

What do the adult saxophone student and music teacher do together?

Consensual sax.

Professor Julliardo: What do you do if the pitch of your anvil is too sharp for Verdi's *Anvil Chorus*?

Student: Toss it out of the pit orchestra, or pound it with a hammer to flatten it.

What is the difference between a concert band and a symphonic band?

The effort made by the musicians. Those in a concert band make a concerted effort whereas the efforts made by those in the symphonic band seem phony.

Why do some people have bagpipes in the front seat of their car?

Because they don't have air bags.

How are a drum set kit and a vacuum cleaner the same?

They both have dirt bags in them.

Why are conductors' hearts coveted for transplants?

They've had so little use.

Band manager: What is the difference between a B-flat clarinet and an alto clarinet?

Clarinetist: $15.00 an hour.

Professor Julliardo: Just let the music flow out smoothly. Make it look easy.

Saxophone student: That's easy for you to say!

You won't believe what happened on my way to a Rolling Stones concert!

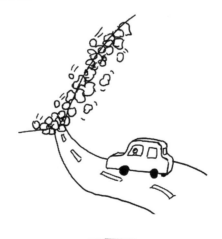

How are a banjo and a vacuum cleaner different?

> You have to plug in the vacuum cleaner before it sucks.

What is the difference between an old lawnmower and a new accordion?

> If you put both of them in the give-away ads, you will get rid of the lawnmower.

What can you find on both a string bass and in Brooklyn?

> A bridge.

Why did the chicken cross the road?

> To get away from the bassoon recital.

Why should you avoid string players?

> Because they're prone to violins.

What does an organized group of musicians need?

> Band-aid.

How does a violist play a very long note?

> Ties one bow to the end of another.

John: Know what I'm gonna do for you?

Mary: No, what?

John: Play *Night and Day* for you on my accordion.

Mary: Oh, pleeeease don't do that!

John: Why not?

Mary: You need to get some sleep every night and so do I.

Harvey: Our band is in trouble. We lost six musicians.

Jack: So, why is that a problem?

Harvey: We had a seven-piece band.

During online Zoom instruction, the teacher asked each of her students to play a piece of music she had mailed to them last week to practice. They played one at a time, listening to the other parts to see how their parts fit in. Part way through, the teacher could not hear the trumpet player. She asked him why he wasn't playing now even though he was still holding his horn up. He replied, "It says on my music to use the mute now, so I hit the mute button on my computer."

What is A-sharp minor?

   (a) The one who gets out of the mine before the
   canary dies.

   (b) The one who finds a vein of gold, but doesn't
   tell anyone until after he buys stock in the
   mining company.

And what is A-sharp major?

   A candidate for colonel.

At the start of Henry Cowell's *Shoonthree*, there is an oboe solo, followed by a flute solo, and then a soprano sax solo. All three play a similar pattern of notes. After the concert, the oboist comes up to the sax player and says, "You rushed the first measure of your solo." The sax player responds, "But it was no problem. I ended at just the right time since I slowed down for the rest of the solo." The oboist looks confused and mutters, "But...but...." The sax player reassures the oboist that there is no problem. "As a sax player, I have been granted unconditional permission by God to improvise whenever I feel like it, but oboists always must play precisely what is written!"

What did the police officer sing to keep people from going back into a burning house?

   "Smoke Gets in Your Eyes."

Why did the police officer arrest the viola player?

   Because he was a violator

Some Places for Musicians to Live

Belfast, Maine

Big Bow, Kansas

Carol Stream, Illinois

Drummond, Idaho

Flatwoods, Tennessee

High Rock, North Carolina

Largo, Florida

Pickens, Mississippi

Reed, Kentucky

Rock Hall, Maryland

Rocklin, California

Scales Mounds, Illinois

Viola, Wyoming

Woodsville, New Hampshire

Patricia H. Wheeler

How can you help homeless people learn new skills?

Toss your old band instruments into the dumpster.

Will this help them get off the street?

People will pay them not to play, but they will probably still be homeless.

New band member: Hey buddy, how late does the band play?

Fellow musician: Oh, about half a beat behind the drummer.

Patient: Will I be able to play trumpet when I get my dentures?

Dentist: Sure, as long as you wear your dentures when you are playing.

Patient: That's weird. I couldn't play trumpet with my real teeth.

What's the difference between the range of a tenor tuba and a contrabass tuba?

About ten yards.

Why do the drummers have a half-ounce larger brains than the horses?

So they will be less likely to disgrace the band in the parade.

Some Vehicles for Musicians

Austin Allegro

Cord

Flat Linea

Ford Supercrew

Isuzu Bellel

Nissan Touring

Piper Cub

Rockne

Toyota Echo

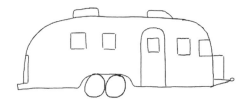

Air Stream Trailer

At rehearsal one evening, the conductor wanted the band to work on a challenging section of a piece and said. "Everyone go to P." Half the band members got up and headed to the restrooms.

Why are trombone players poor managers?

Because they tend to let everything slide.

Musician: I have four quarter notes in the third measure after G, but there should be only three since we're in 3/4.

Conductor: Just play them faster!

What is the difference between a mouse and a clarinet?

You can't hear a mouse squeak when the band is playing.

The clarinet section leader was assigning three parts to the players. Jim, you're on first. I'll be on second. Chris, you go to third. Chris asks, "Is this a band rehearsal or a baseball game?"

How do you tune these horns?

An Alphorn—if flat, go up the mountain; if sharp, go down the mountain.

A French Horn—try a new twist.

An English Horn—it should have been tuned at the factory.

Two drummers were chatting in back. The conductor says, "I haven't given a downbeat and you're already too loud."

What happened to a drummer who just got kicked out by his roommate?

He became homeless.

Why should we pity the piccolo player who swallowed an apricot pit?

Because the pit-too-lo.

If My Radio Is Too Loud,
Please Forgive Me.
I'm a Rock Drummer.

The conductor tells the bass drummer that he is playing too fast. The bass drummer asks, "What tempo do you suggest?" Another band member quietly says, "Senior citizen tempo. They're the ones who come to hear our concerts."

When the circus parade went by Buckingham Palace, who was the escort for the Queen?

Band Master Karl L. King.

Teaching on-line can be a challenge, especially with background noise. One student was playing some exercises that the teacher had assigned to her. She was accompanied by her dog, howling in the background. This is a problem that can't be solved by hitting the mute button. And the dog did not want to go outside as he liked "singing" to the music.

Patricia H. Wheeler

Why are trombone players auditioned at the playground?

To see if they can use the slide and know how to swing.

One student was playing a march on his clarinet for his teacher in an on-line class. But he seemed to have a percussionist accompanying him. It turned out to be his dog, hitting its tail against the dog crate in rhythm to the music. Maybe this dog can join our percussion section when we are back in school. We need percussionists with a good sense of rhythm.

Should Have Brought a Fly Swatter.

15

Sempre Humor

>

Which is longer, the C-flute or the alto flute?

They look like they're the same length, but that's because the alto flute player has larger hands and wider shoulders.

How can a deaf person tell if a trombone is out-of-tune?

She can see the slide moving.

What is the difference between a euphonium and a tuba?

The tuba holds the ashes of more conductors.

Student: How can I tell when my mouthpiece needs cleaning?

Professor Julliardo: When it smells like a dead rat.

What do you get when you cross a computer and a cymbal?

A computer that crashes every time you touch it.

Dying husband to his wife: When I die, will you get married again?

Wife: Oh, I couldn't do that. I love you too much.

Husband: Well, don't you like being married?

Wife: Of course I do.

Husband: Well, then you should think about getting married again. I wouldn't want you all by yourself.

Wife: Well, I'll think about it.

Husband: Well, if you get married again, would you let him drive my car?

Wife: Yeh, probably. It's in pretty good running shape.

Husband: Would you make lasagna for him like you do for me?

Wife: Sure, if he likes my recipe.

Husband: Would you let him use my fishing poles?

Wife: Of course, if he likes to fish.

Husband: Would you let him sleep in bed with you?

Wife: Well, if I were married to him, sure, why not.

Husband: Would you let him use my drum set?

Wife: Oh, no way. He has no sense of rhythm.

Some Places for Musicians to Live

Bel Air, Maryland

Belleville, New Jersey

Blair, Wisconsin

Bowers Beach, Delaware

Fort Rock, Oregon

Harper, Washington

High Rolls, New Mexico

Keyes, Oklahoma

Landrum, South Carolina

Ringtown, Pennsylvania

Rockwell City, Iowa

Slick Rock, Colorado

Speed, West Virginia

Woods, Kansas

How are a bass sax and a euphonium alike?

> Both are made of brass, but one is a bass saxophone and the other is a bass saxhorn. Sounds like they are cousins.

What is the difference between a conductor and a bag of dog food?

> The bag, and people will pay for the bag of dog food.

What is a big country hit?

> Smashing into a 275-pound sousaphone player on a rural road.

What is an organ donor?

> One who gives old organs to churches.

And what do you call someone who switches the organs?

> A surgeon.

Why do piccolo players like dachshunds for pets?

> Because the dogs can carry their owners' instruments on their backs.

Student: Why did Elgar entitled his work *Pomp and Circumstance* when graduation is a *Circumstance for Pomp*?

Professor Julliardo: Do you expect to graduate if you ask dumb questions like that?

One evening, both the concert band and the orchestra were performing at the same time in nearby theaters. The band's conductor was worried about having a large enough audience and, when it was time to start, his worries were realized. The audience was smaller than the number of players in the band. But he informed the audience that they had made the right choice coming to the band's concert instead of going to the orchestra's performance. He said, "You are really going to enjoy this evening—lots of sax and no violins!"

What can you find on a string bass and under your bathroom sink?

A tailpiece.

Why did the middle-school students name their band the Nosy Players?

Because they all had a little boogie.

—

Driving to different gigs, a tuba player and a trumpet player hit each other head on. Both climbed out of their cars, relieved to see that the other driver appeared to be okay. The trumpet player said, "Look at those cars. We should celebrate not getting killed in this crash!" The tuba player replied, "Great idea. I have a bottle of bourbon in the car." "Get it," responded the trumpet player, "and have a good swallow." The tuba player opened the bottle and took five good gulps. Handing the bottle to the trumpet player, he said, "Here you go. Now you can celebrate." "I'll wait 'til the police get here," tooted the trumpeter.

—

What do you get if you cross a kazoo and an onion?

A noisemaker that brings tears to your eyes.

—

What technique do percussionists use for birth control?

The rhythm method, but it would work better if they could count.

—

What did Professor Julliardo say when his new student asked him where to start?

"Begin the Beguine."

—

Where does the spit go? Match the place with the instrument.

(1) Drips onto your feet	(a) Trombone
(2) Gathers in the butt joint	(b) Piccolo
(3) Collects in a puddle in your bell	(c) Harmonica
(4) Falls into your neighbor's lap	(d) Horn
(5) Drips into your lap and down your leg	(e) Flute
(6) Falls onto your shoulder and runs down your arm	(f) Bassoon
(7) Drizzles down the neck of the person in front of you	(g) Sax
(8) Flies into the back of the head of the person in front of you	(h) Tuba
(9) Plops onto the head of your instrument	(i) Clarinet, Oboe
(10) Gets all over your hands	(j) Trumpet
(11) Goes into the u-tube	(k) Drum
(12) Runs down your chin and neck	(l) Electric guitar
(13) Drizzles into your lap	(m) Contrabassoon

Answers: 1—i, 2—f, 3—g, 4—e, 5—d, 6—b, 7—a, 8—j, 9—k, 10—c, 11-m, 12—l, 13—h

If you wear a toupee, don't sit in front of a trombone player.

What do a contrabass tuba and the digestive track have in common?

They both make deep, gurgling sounds and they need a long stretch of unclogged tubing to work properly.

What did the reviewer say about the symphony's performance?

Concert-o-gross-o!

What do you have when a really lousy saxophonist plays "Harlem Nocturne"?

A Harlem nightmare.

What do you call a bunch of clarinet and sax players just before a concert?

Cane suckers.

What is the difference between a dead trombonist in the road and a dead country western singer in the road?

The length of the slide marks in front of the trombonist.

Some Vehicles for Musicians

Dodge Cornet

Ford Windstar

Morris Major

Piper GTT/P2

Pontiac Firebird

Rock 'n Roll Tandem Bike

Solo (Chinese car model)

Wright Fusion Bus

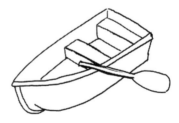

Dinghy

Patricia H. Wheeler

Mary, the harpist, and Sam, the trombonist, went out one evening before rehearsal to a local discotheque. Sam's car wouldn't lock, but Sam knew Fran, the owner, so they locked their instruments in Fran's office. Having had too much to drink, they went to rehearsal without their instruments. When the conductor noticed that Mary didn't have her instrument, he asked her where it was, to which she replied, "I left my harp in Sam's Fran's disco."

Why do sax players wear neck straps?

So they can blame their poor playing on a maladjusted neck strap.

What equipment does a musical chef have on hand?

Tuning fork, chopping block, serenaded knife, T-bone steaks, cup, sharp knife, flat skillet.

Betty had tuned up her timpani and Frank his string bass. They headed back to the dressing rooms prior to the entire orchestra taking their seats for their spring concert. As the conductor walked onto the stage with the audience clapping, Betty and Frank got in place to play their parts. Frank suddenly realized his bow wasn't on his music stand where he left it. He asked Betty if she knew where it was. Betty replied, "Oh no! It's in the women's dressing room. I took it in there to use as a back scratcher." "Well," exclaimed Frank, "Now all I can play are the plucking parts."

What do doctors in Tennessee call a bad cold?

"The Chattanoog-a Choo Choo."

Top ten reasons to hire a bagpiper:

(10) You want to see a guy in a skirt.

(9) You want to show others how bad music can be so they will appreciate your playing.

(8) Plaids are in.

(7) You want to chase the dogs out of your yards.

(6) You want people to leave your party early.

(5) You want to see if other people's knees are as ugly as yours.

(4) You want to drive the drug dealers out of the neighborhood.

(3) You can't afford a real musician.

(2) You want people to volunteer to play at your next party to save money.

(1) The harmonica player was already booked.

16

In Memory

fine

Where is Felix Mendelssohn?

Trying to find his way out of *Fingal's Cave*.

What is Elvis Presley doing?

Shakin' and twistin' with the lonesome *Hound Dog* on the steps of the *Heartbreak Hotel*.

What is Ferde Grofé up to?

Riding a mule in the Grand Canyon.

What is Richard Wagner looking for from heaven?

The Flying Dutchman.

What does Ella Fitzgerald say she's doing?

I'm Beginning to See the Light.

What is Franz Schubert up to?

Trying to catch five trout for his *Trout Quintet.*

What is Jerry Garcia seeking?

More deadheads who are grateful to him.

Where is Oscar Hammerstein II?

Vacationing in the *South Pacific.*

How has Louis Armstrong changed?

Ain't Misbehavin' anymore.

What is Tommy Dorsey doing?

Taking a *Sentimental Journey*.

What is Nikolai Rimsky-Korsakov up to?

Buzzing with the bumble bees.

What is Marian Anderson still doing?

Reminding us that a Black woman can be a fabulous music teacher and opera singer.

Where is Karl King?

Sitting in *The Big Cage* while watching *Barnum and Bailey's Favorite* circus acts.

What is Stephen Foster doing?

Relaxing on a paddle wheeler on the Mississippi River with the *Old Folks at Home*.

Where is Antonín Dvořák?

Going Home from *The New World*.

What is Franz Léhar doing?

Waltzing with *The Merry Widow*.

What is Glenn Miller up to?

Looking for his gal in Kalamazoo.

What is Jim Christensen doing?

Enjoying a *Fantasy in the Sky*.

What is Billie Holiday doing?

Singing the blues.

What is Peter Ilyich Tchaikovsky doing?

Trying to wake up *Sleeping Beauty*.

What sound is Henry Fillmore making?

Rolling Thunder in the sky.

What is Leonard Bernstein looking for?

A good West Side Story.

Where is John Lennon?

Playing in the Lonely Hearts Club Band.

What is George Gershwin doing?

Trying to drive in London town on A Foggy Day.

What is Aaron Copland doing?

Taking a hike in May on the Appalachian Trail.

What is Carl Maria von Weber up to?

Trying to find someone to accept an Invitation to the Dance.

What is Hoagy Carmichael up to?

Floating up a Lazy River, singing Heart and Soul.

Where is Woody Guthrie?

Doing some Hard Travelin'.

What does Gioacchino Rossini want to find?

The Barber of Seville to cut his hair.

Where is Frédéric Chopin?

Lying heartless in Paris under Polish soil while composing more piano études.

What is Richard Rodgers doing?

Riding on a Carousel in Oklahoma.

Whom is Hector Berlioz searching for?

> Looking in Italy for Harold so they can go to the *Roman Carnival* together.

What is Bedřich Smetana doing?

> Spreading smetana (sour cream) across the sky.

What is Igor Stravinsky up to?

> Cruising in his *Firebird*.

What is Jimi Hendrix up to?

> Going *Up From The Skies* to see a *Foxey Lady*.

Where is Benny Goodman?

> *Stompin' at the Savoy*.

What is Kate Smith doing in heaven?

> Belting out *God Bless America*.

Where is Edvard Grieg?

> Marching in the funeral parade for Rikard Nodraak.

What is Frank Sinatra able to do now?

> Hold *The World on a String*.

What is Fred Jewell up to now?

> Strolling as an *Easy Walker* with the *High and Mighty*.

What is Johannes Brahms doing?

> Singing lullabies.

Where has Modest Mussorgsky gone?

> Camping over-*Night on Bald Mountain*.

Where is Giacomo Puccini?

> Hanging out with Bohemian artists on the Left Bank of the Seine River.

What is Mary Martin doing now?

> Providing *The Sound of Music* over the *South Pacific*.

What is Victor Herbert doing?

> Hanging out with *Naughty Marietta* in *The Red Mill* and looking at *Babes in Toyland*.

What is Ludwig van Beethoven doing?

Listening to what people are saying about his works.

What is Bing Crosby doing now?

Looking for *Pennies From Heaven*.

How does Wolfgang Amadeus Mozart get to sleep?

By listening to *A Little Night Music*.

Where is Russell Alexander?

Standing tall next to the *Colossus of Columbia*.

What is Duke Ellington doing?

Looking for a *Sophisticated Lady*.

Where is John Denver?

Leaving on a Jet Plane for his *Rocky Mountain High*.

What is Harold Arlen doing?

Somewhere Over the Rainbow looking for the *Paper Moon*.

What is Helen Reddy telling us?

Reminding us she is a woman as she sings *Ain't No Way to Treat a Lady*.

What is "Little Richard" Wayne Penniman doing now?

Rockin' and rollin' in heaven.

What can Ellis Marsalis Jr. do for us now?

Brighten things up for us through the solar corona now that COVID-19 has taken him away from us.

What is something only Eddie Van Halen can do?

Electrifying heaven as he plays *Jump* in the clouds.

What is Ennio Morricone busy doing?

> Going around with *A Fistful of Dollars* to dole out to *The Good, The Bad, and The Ugly.*

What is Charley Pride doing each day in heaven?

> Singing *Kiss an Angel Good Morning.*

What is Johnny Nash doing?

> Singing *I Can See Clearly Now* since he has a great view from heaven.

Where is Henry Mancini?

> Looking for *The Pink Panther* along *Moon River.*

What is Viola Smith's mission in heaven?

> Telling us to "Give Girl Musicians A Break" as she plays her drums in a way few male drummers can do.

What can John Prine do now that he's in heaven?

> After dying of COVID -19, now he can meet the *Angel from Montgomery.* But before going to heaven, he recorded *I Remember Everything* for the soundtrack of the COVID-19 memorial video played at the first night of the 2020 Democratic National Convention.

What do people want to know about Leroy Anderson?

> If composing *Sleigh Ride* during a July heat wave was a way to keep him cool.

What is Dave Brubeck doing in heaven?

> Reminding us to *Take Five* and do it *In Your Own Sweet Way.*

Patricia H. Wheeler

Where are Alan Jay Lerner and Frederick Loewe now?

In *Camelot*.

What is Nat "King" Cole doing now?

Showing us how to *Get Your Kicks On Route 66* while looking for the *Ramblin' Rose*.

What did Scott Joplin do?

Gave us ragtime with *Maple Leaf Rag*, *The Entertainer*, and more.

What is Charlie Parker doing now?

Providing bebop in heaven with his saxophone.

What did Clara and Robert Schumann do?

Provided compositions of Romanticism based on their love for each other.

What is Giuseppe Verdi up to?

Enjoying a *Falstaff* beer.

What did Ray Charles do?

> Showed us what soul music is and that even if you're blind you can compose and play music.

What is John Philip Sousa doing now?

> Marching around heaven with all the musicians he can round up.

What has Michael Jackson done?

> Moved from Neverland to Everland.

What is Bob Marley up to now?

> Wailing from above with the other two Wailers.

What is Mama Cass Elliot telling us?

> Letting us know there's a *New World Coming*.

Why is Fanny Mendelssohn Hensel happy?

> She's pleased that she's finally getting credit for composing the *Easter Sonata*.

What is John Coltrane doing?

> Bebop-ping in the sky.

17

Symbols that Musicians Need to Know

♯	Go up a half step, but stay in your seat.
Opt	Can ad lib or sit out.
$	Pay to play.
>	Tongue the note hard.
esc	Go backstage and hide.
//	A railroad crossing, so stop and look at the conductor before proceeding.
:‖	Repeat, maybe.

$\boldsymbol{f}$	Play loudly.
$\boldsymbol{ff}$	Go fast forward.
$\boldsymbol{fff}$	Go fast forward to the fine.
$\boldsymbol{mf}$	Play much faster.
$\boldsymbol{p}$	Play quietly.
$\boldsymbol{pp}$	What to do during intermission.
!	Watch the conductor.
zzz	Take a rest.
,	Gasp for air.
~	Turn, but don't hit the person next to you.
‖	Stop playing.
Tutti	Toot your horn.
2x	This part is x-rated the second time it's played.
D2	It says that the second person to arrive is the designated drummer.
440	Take this Interstate to get to Music Row in Nashville.

Patricia H. Wheeler

Glossary

Abbandono—an unemployed, divorced musician who is kicked out of the homeless shelter.

Accelerando—put the pedal to the metal.

Accent—what many Texas musicians have.

Accidentals—notes that don't blend in too well with the rest of the band.

Acoustic guitar—a long, thin guitar that is good for playing billiards.

Aeolian mode—the way you like grandma's apple pie.

Agitato—a clarinet player's emotional state when the reed splits.

Air—what some musicians can never get enough of and others seem to have too much of.

Alto trombone—a very weak tenor trombone.

Altos—ten toes used for counting rests.

Amplifier—a deliverer of unpleasant, even painful, feedback.

Andante—a musical composition that is infernally slow.

Antiphonal—referring to the prohibition of cell phones during the concert.

Anvil—a leftover item from the school's metal shop class that's given to the band.

Arpeggio—a musical version of an archipelago.

Ascending scales—a cobra rising up to the music of the snake charmer's oboe.

Aubade—the music critic's description of a lousy performance.

Audience—a group of people, most of whom have gathered in a given place to be seen for purely social reasons.

Augmented fifth—a quart.

Bach chorale—the place behind the barn where you keep the horses.

Ballad—promotional piece for spherical sports items.

Bar Line—what musicians get into after a gig.

Baroque—musicians when they pay their bills each month.

Bass—what musicians want to catch on their days off.

Bass clef—where you'll end up if you fall off the edge of a cliff.

Bassoon—what a fisherman hopes for.

Bind—what a soloist who hasn't practiced is in on opening night.

Block—a stretch walked many times by musicians on strike.

Blues—a condition suffered by musicians when their paychecks bounce.

Bombardo—the entry of all brass players at once while playing fortissimo.

Bop—getting hit on the head by a flying drum stick.

Bow—a bright ribbon tied on the end of a trombone slide so that people can see it coming.

Breve—a sustained note until your fingers slip off the keys or you run out of air.

Cadenza—a piece of furniture to pile sheet music on.

Canon—the instrument every tuba play dreams of owning.

CD—an LP that wasn't given steroids.

Cello—a 100-year-old gelatin dessert.

Chamber—music played in court to help the prosecution and defense come to an agreement.

Chant—what students are doing when the music teacher arrives late.

Character—a term describing many musicians we all know personally.

Chorale—a place to herd musicians.

Chord—a device used to tie a bass drum to the top of a pickup truck.

Cipher—a volunteer musician.

Clef—what you try to never fall off of.

Close harmony—soprano saxophones in unison.

Common chord—the one everybody in the band knows.

Con velocità—hit the accelerator.

Concave pedals—ones you can sink your feet into.

Concert pitch—the note tossed out prior to the start of a concert.

Concerto Grossissimo—a really bad performance.

Conductor—a person who can follow many musicians at the same time.

Console—(1) the part of the organ that kittens walk on. (2) to stroke gently and say kind words to musicians.

Cool—music that's not so hot.

Counterpoint—two sides of an argument.

Counting—a skill most drummers lack.

Crab movement—a technique for a grouch to get away from the drum corps show.

Crash—the sound made when the violinist backs up and knocks over the hanging chimes.

Crook—(1) the musician's second job needed for survival. (2) the burglary tool that a bassoon player uses to steal for a living.

Debile—excretion from the liver.

Degree—something earned by some musicians that makes it even harder for them to find work.

Delicato—impossibility for bass drummers.

Détaché—(1) a type of trombone whose slide keeps falling off. (2) the band member who was laid off.

Diatonic—a calorie-free drink.

Diminished fifth—An almost empty bottle of Johnny Walker.

Discreto—the method which the band manager must use to handle conflicts within the trumpet section.

Disperato—the way the band manager feels two hours before the concert and the conductor is sick.

Divisi—in-fighting within a section of the band.

Drum roll—what happens when the bass drum falls off the flatbed truck in the parade.

Dynamics—mysterious squiggles in the music that only the conductor understands.

Electric tuner—a device that rarely agrees with you.

Elevato—a lift for Italian musicians.

Embouchure—a version of standard American English that means, "I am certain."

Energico—the result of eating a candy bar during intermission.

Execution—plans for the conductor.

Exercise—marching band practice.

Expressive organ—pounding heart.

Fine—relief for all.

Flag—how conductors try to get musicians' attention.

Flat—a tired musician.

Flat minor—a child under a piano.

Forte—where the cavalry band hides from the Indians.

Fortissimo—a trumpet player's mezzo-piano.

Frets—what a soloist does before going on stage.

Furioso—what a conductor becomes when you miss one or more 32nd notes in five measures at 176 beats per minute.

Ges dur—the concert hall entry for distinguished guests.

Glee—the feeling students have when their music lesson is over.

Glissando—(1) a flutist's technique for difficult runs. (2) the sound a trombonist makes when the slide falls off. (3) a musician on ice.

Grave—a final resting place for musicians.

Grosso—a description of the place where the spit goes.

Half step—two piccolos playing in unison.

Harmony—the desired state of affairs in the band.

Harp—how music teachers remind students to practice.

Head—the top of the drum and of the drummer.

Horn band—a herd of bulls.

Improvisation—saxophonists' excuse for playing something other than what is written.

Instrumental hit—getting whacked by a trombone slide.

Jam session—lunchtime with peanut butter sandwiches.

Key change sign—a notation that half the band misses every time.

Key pad—home base for traveling musicians.

Klang—sound made when the drummer knocks over the gong.

Largo—the biggest musician in the band.

Legato—the marching band.

Lunga—what is used to take in a deep breath.

Lyre—a student who tells his teacher he practices four hours each day.

Major scale—a 30-step stairway that a musician has to haul his tuba up so he can get to the stage.

Medley—the results of someone meddling around with other people's music.

Melodic minor—a child who sings well.

Metronome—(1) a subway pixie. (2) a device that drummers don't know how to use.

Minor second—younger child who sings in unison with an older child.

Modern music—music that the audience doesn't recognize and can't decide if they like it or not.

Mouth organ—tongue.

Movement—what constipated musicians want to have.

Moving notes—what you see when you look at your music and have floaters in your eyes.

Mute—a silencer.

Natural minor scale—the first seven notes that a young beginning brass player makes.

New Age Music—(1) music that is so hypnotic you think you really like it. (2) music that sounds just as bad whether you play it forwards or backwards.

Notehead—the band's nerd.

Notes—messages to parents from the music teacher that students lose on the way home.

Obilgato—you had better not mess up this part!

Oboe—a cockney tramp.

Oder—what you get when a student opens his instrument case from last year on the first day of school.

Opus—what a guitarist says when her finger is infected.

Pad saver—on-time rent payment.

Pastorale—to be played out in the countryside, where no one will hear you.

Perfect pitch—(1) throwing a piccolo into the toilet without hitting the rim. (2) throwing a banjo into the dumpster and hitting the accordion straight on. (3) the ability to hear someone else out of tune, but not yourself.

Pianissimo—a tiny piano.

Pizzicato—(1) an incontinent pet. (2) music that is a piece of cake. (3) popular Italian menu item.

Progression—that which the music teacher hopes students make.

Pulse—what a string player does to make strings pizzicato.

Quarter note—what the coach gives to the quarterback at the end of each quarter.

Quarter tone—half the maximum load for a half-ton pickup truck.

Quasi—how your stomach feels after playing two hours of modern music.

Quaver—the natural vibrato produced by an old brass player's lips.

Redundant—the title brass players give to the part played over and over again by the woodwind players in band rehearsal while they wait.

Refrain—(1) a sudden downpour that ends your neighborhood park concert. (2) the few words of a popular song that everyone knows. (3) what falls when the drummer's marijuana bag breaks on a windy day.

Relative major—a brother in the Army.

Relative minor—a musician's child.

Repeat—directions to practice this strain again until you get it right, then you can go on.

Recess—the reason for intermission.

Ritardando—a condition suffered by many drummers.

Rock—an item thrown at musicians by the audience when they have a bad performance.

Schwer—music that makes players schweat.

Score—(1) rating by music critics. (2) acquiring a new instrument. (3) finding a reed that works.

Segue—a two-wheel device that a street musician can use to get away from trouble.

Senza sordino—when you dropped your mute and it rolls off the stage.

Shake—what happens with your music stand during an earthquake, when there is a loud drum roll, or when a trumpet player blasts out noise that make the audience tremble.

Sharp—the type of jokester that every band needs.

Sheet music—what musicians sleep on.

Show stopper—what occurs when the soloist faints.

Simile—keep doing what you were doing, even if the conductor doesn't like it.

Skip—what musicians occasionally do to a line of music.

Slur—technique for blending in when you make a late entry.

Soft pedal—pianist who isn't wearing shoes.

Solo—about as far down as one can go.

Sordino—(1) stuff a fish in your horn. (2) sound fishy and salty.

Sound hole—period when the microphone is off, but should be on.

Space—that which the band never seems to have enough of on stage or room in their cases for their instruments.

Spianato—jump out of your chair!

Spitzflöte—a flute that constantly drizzles.

Square time—practice session with a bunch of nerds.

Step—something that musicians trip on when trying to get on stage.

Stinger—the piccolo player's solo when the rest of the band is done.

Stopped notes—(1) those collected by the music teacher when students try to pass them around during band practice. (2) those with a fermata that are cut off quickly by the conductor. (3) the technique that French horn players use to imitate an English horn sound.

Stopped pipes—the tracheas of singers with bronchitis.

Strain—(1) what oboe players always seem to do when they are playing. (2) a common occupational hazard among music teachers.

Stretch—(1) how harpists reach the lowest strings. (2) an attempt to understand a musical definition, explanation, joke, or modern music.

String quartet—a proficient violinist, a lousy violinist, a wanna-be violinist, and one who despises violins.

Subtonic—cheap tonic water.

Swell—what parents think of their children in the school's band concert.

Swing—what drummers do with sticks.

Tambourine—a device for measuring the severity of spasms.

Temperament—the conductor's personality, usually nasty.

Tempo—a car that a drummer thinks he can afford, but has difficulty keeping up with the payments.

Tempo di Marcia—play at the same rate that Marcia is playing.

Timbre—French logs, that is, what trees turn into when you blast a French horn in the forest.

Tonic—Something to mix with gin.

Trascinando—(1) a disposable piece of music. (2) optional.

Treble—what you get into when you don't practice.

Tremolo—the precursor of an earthquake set off by the percussion section.

Trombone—a manually-operated, wind-driven, pitch approximator.

Tuning hammer—what your conductor will hit you with if you're out of tune.

Tutti—the sound of the flute.

Upbeats—stretching exercises for the conductor.

Vacillando—play or don't play, depending on your mood.

Velocissimo—the way to drive when late for a gig.

Virtuoso—a musician who pays the composer to add a strain at the end of a piece so he can play a solo at the concert and add it to his resume.

Whole note—a note with a hole printed in the middle of it.

Whole tone—the sound made by blowing across an open hole.

Wind—the reason all band members carry clothes pins for the summer season.

Woodwind quintet—a flutist, an oboist, a clarinetist, a bassoonist, and a French horn player who are too stuffy to play with the rest of the band, but can put up with each other. And since when is a French horn a woodwind instrument?

Epilogue

THE COVID-19 BLUES
(A Musician's Lament)
By Tony Altwies © 2021

Oh Covid, oh Covid, now what did you do?
The music is gone and the days are so blue.
We distance so far that sounds cannot blend,
As YouTube and Zoom aren't musicians' friends.

All harmony is gone with masking profound,
Where even our fingers sanitize the sound.
Our chops diminish with quarantine abound,
While our horns lay dormant, so lost and not found.

The '20 Pandemic will historically go down,
Not only with fever, but a musical frown.
Nary has such as COVID been the cause,
To give all live music such a fatal pause.

While the coda is near as we segue a chord,
Our melody's as clear as the stream is to ford.
Our score nears its end and we find the repeat.
We now must refuse to contemplate defeat.

Vaccinate, Vaccinate, Vaccinate's the plan.
Pfizer or Moderna—get one if you can!
Our goal is as fleeting as the song of a bird,
Ever chasing immunity in the form of a herd.

About the Author

Patricia H. Wheeler began playing clarinet in fifth grade until her orthodontist suggested she change to flute because of her overbite. She continued playing flute through junior and senior high school and as an undergraduate. Since she had played clarinet a little, her music teacher asked her to help teach saxophone for a year in high school, which is when she picked up a curved soprano sax. For marching band in college, she was asked to also play piccolo. After college, she took several years off until her younger son's teacher advised him to join the Pleasanton Community Concert Band so he would feel more challenged. Since he was in eighth grade and she had to drive him to and from rehearsals and concerts, Pat unburied her flute and joined also. To this day, she continues playing flute and piccolo in local community bands.

She has played with many musical groups. These include five local community bands—Danville Community Band, Ohlone Community Band, Pleasanton Community Concert Band, San Ramon Symphonic Band, and Tracy Community Band. She did not play with all of these at the same time though, as there are only so many nights in the week to go to rehearsals. She has also played on several occasions with the Association of Concert Bands' Convention Band, the Castro Valley High School Reunion Band, Flute Fest (a local flute choir), the Nevada County Invitational Concert Band, the Williamsburg Consort, the Windjammers Circus Band, and more. She has gone on international tours with Community Bands at Sea and with the North Suburban Concert Band from Minnesota.

She is a member of the Honorary Arts Commission of the Livermore Valley Performing Arts Center and of the board of the Livermore-Amador Symphony Guild. For ten years, she was on the board of the Friends of the Golden Gate Park Band and for 20 years on the board of the Pleasanton Community Concert Band. She also was on the board of Windjammers Unlimited for four years.

Besides music and family, her other passion is being a therapy dog handler. Her four dogs have done over 4,000 hours of visits and all have earned the American Kennel Club (AKC) Therapy Dog Distinguished title. She is a tester/observer for the Alliance of Therapy Dogs and has assessed over 200 potential teams in the San Francisco Bay Area. She has written two books and many articles about therapy dogs, and given several presentations on this topic.

Dr. Wheeler completed her bachelor's degree in psychology and her master's degree in counseling at the University of Rochester, her MBA in Management at Armstrong College in Berkeley, California, and her PhD in education/policy analysis at the University of California, Berkeley. For over 40 years, she was an educational researcher and evaluator, testing program administrator, and consultant. She is a member of the Tri-Valley Branch of the California Writers' Club.

She has two sons and four grandchildren. When time permits, she loves to travel and has been to about 50 countries and all but one continent (Australia).